MINDFULNESS & SELF-COMPASSION

WORKBOOK FOR KIDS, VOLUME 2

Quest Map
Values
Self-Compassion
Self-Acceptance
Courage
Magic Mountains
Celebration
Comfort
Connection
Imagination
Freedom
Sunshine
Mindfulness
Foundation Forest
Sensations
Acceptance
Sweet Meadow
Kindness
Curiosity
Friendship

MINDFULNESS & SELF-COMPASSION

40+ Fun Activities & Comics to Grow Resilience, Courage, and Compassion

Written by Jamie Lynn Tatera, MS

Foreword by Kristin Neff, PhD

Illustrations by Alyssa Brown and Alexis Warshall

Published in the United States by Wholly Mindful, LLC.

Wholly Mindful and Resilience Habits are trademarks of Wholly Mindful, LLC.
Milwaukee, WI.

The Mindfulness and Self-Compassion Workbook for Kids has been adapted from the Mindfulness and Self-Compassion for Children and Caregivers and the Path to Resilience programs, developed by Jamie Lynn Tatera. The Mindfulness and Self-Compassion for Children and Caregivers program is an adaptation of the Mindful Self-Compassion program created by Christopher Germer and Kristin Neff, who granted permission to use the adapted material for this workbook.

For more information, or to book an event, visit www.jamielynntatera.com.

Library of Congress Cataloging-in-Publication data is available.
ISBN 978-1-952848-06-3 (PB)
Ebook ISBN 978-1-952848-07-0

For children everywhere.
Including You.
You are a gift.

This book belongs to:

____

Table of Contents

FOREWORD BY DR. KRISTIN NEFF

Children today face many challenges, and more than ever they need inner resources that help them meet life's ups and downs with kindness and courage.

In the first volume of this series, children were introduced to the three core elements of self-compassion: mindfulness, common humanity, and kindness. This second volume builds on that foundation by showing them how to use self-compassion in moments of struggle—when big feelings arise and life feels hard.

In this story we meet a new character, Flame the dragon, who sometimes feels worried, angry, or ashamed. Like so many children, Flame is learning how to be with these difficult emotions in a safe and caring way. With guidance from the resilience animals, Flame discovers that compassion has two complementary sides: gentle and strong. Gentle self-compassion helps us soothe and comfort ourselves when we're hurting, while strong self-compassion gives us the courage to protect, stand up for, and support ourselves when needed. Together, these two sides help children face challenges with both tenderness and bravery.

Through creative activities and the authentic voices of children themselves, Jamie Lynn brings essential lessons to life. Kids learn that self-compassion won't make hard things magically disappear, but it *will* help them feel safe, capable, and supported as they get through difficult moments.

As with the first volume, caregivers play a vital role. When adults model self-compassion and practice it alongside children, they show that treating ourselves with kindness is normal, healthy, and wise.

Jamie Lynn's playful yet deeply grounded approach translates the science of self-compassion into a language young hearts can truly feel. I am delighted to celebrate this next step in her work, helping children cultivate both the gentle and the strong compassion they need to flourish.

Dr. Kristin Neff, PhD
Author of Self-Compassion and Fierce Self-Compassion

A Note to Grown-Ups

Welcome! I am so glad you are here. Supporting your child's development of mindfulness and self-compassion skills is a life-changing and empowering gift for your child.

I share my family's story and tips for how to approach this series of books in the introduction to volume one. If you'd like to read the introduction to volume one, you can do so here: https://jamielynntatera.com/workbook-for-kids-resources. Volume 2 of this series can be used as a stand-alone book, but if you find your child lacking foundational mindfulness, connection, and self-kindness skills, I recommend referencing the first volume.

This book is designed to help your child become more aware of their thoughts and feelings, and learn to choose helpful responses when they are struggling. Children are led through eight different "lands" where they playfully learn to focus on joy, navigate worries, grow self-compassion, relate to anger and the inner critic, and motivate themselves to reach for their dreams.

Please approach this journey as a co-learner with your child. Your child may wish to do this workbook with you, or they may wish to do it on their own. Sometimes groups of parents do this workbook together so that they can learn the skills they want their child to grow.

If you have a hard time with some of the practices, you can appropriately share your struggles with your child and model self-compassion practice. Normalizing struggles, including struggles with practicing self-compassion, can help kids do the same.

Once kids are familiar with a practice, you can begin to invite them to practice self-compassion during difficult moments. It usually works best to first provide kids with your comfort and encouragement, and then invite kids to offer comfort to themselves. If your child resists practicing self-compassion, it's best to simply speak to your child with the compassionate voice that you'd like for them to internalize. Your compassionate words and example will help kids develop their own compassionate voice over time.

Finally, be kind to yourself. No parent/caregiver is perfect. You care so much about children (as demonstrated by reading this book!), and you're doing great!

With deep appreciation, gratitude, and joy,
Jamie Lynn

A Note to Kids

Hi I'm Jamie Lynn, and I've created this book with a team of kids! In the previous book, we took the Feelings Habit Animal Quiz.

Find out which of these animals is your feelings habit!!

If you'd like, you can count or tally your quiz answers here. →

a	b	c	d	e

If you haven't taken the playful Feelings Animal Quiz, visit jamielynntatera.com/feelings-habit-animal-quiz or scan the QR code (or ask a grown-up for help).

Chameleon has hidden emotions

Bear has BIG emotions.

Deer is ashamed of difficult emotions.

Beaver keeps thinking about challenging situations

Flame the dragon has all the feeling habits.

When something goes wrong, Flame keeps thinking about it, like Beaver.

Then Flame tries to ignore the difficult feelings and situations, like Chameleon.

Next Flame's feelings come exploding out, like Bear.

Finally, Flame feels shame for having these feelings, like Deer.

The **Resilience Animals** help us learn helpful habits.

Doodles: What do you need to do?

Buddy: You are not alone.

Super Snuggles: I care about you.

Spots: What do you feel and sense?

Sunny: Soak in good things.

Being resilient means we can cope with hard things. The resilience animals help us learn helpful habits, like mindfulness and self-compassion.

Self-compassion is being a friend to yourself when life is hard.

Mindfulness is noticing what is happening in the moment with curiosity.

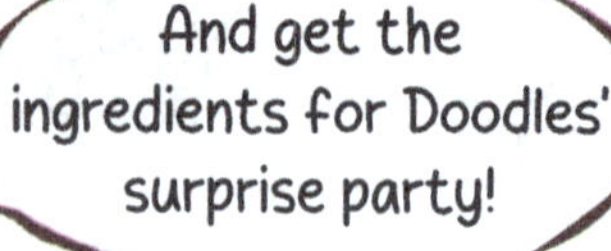

Our quest map was broken in half, so we only did half the adventures in our last book.
Here's the map for the quest. Be careful with it. We need the whole map to gather all of the magical cake ingredients.
Only I should hold the map. I can take care of it perfectly.
NO! I should have the map. Give it to me!!!
Stop fighting or you'll tear the map!
Oh no! I broke it! I've ruined everything.
I don't know how to feel about this.
I found the rest of the map!!
Later Deer found the rest of the map, so now we can finish our quest!

Quest Map
Values
Self-Compassion
Self-Acceptance
Courage
Magic Mountains
Celebration
Comfort
Connection
Imagination
Freedom
You Are Here
Sunshine
Mindfulness
Foundation Forest
Sensations
Sweet Meadow
We went through the first eight lands in book 1. We will pick up our adventure in the Land of Sunshine.
Kindness
Curiosity
Friendship

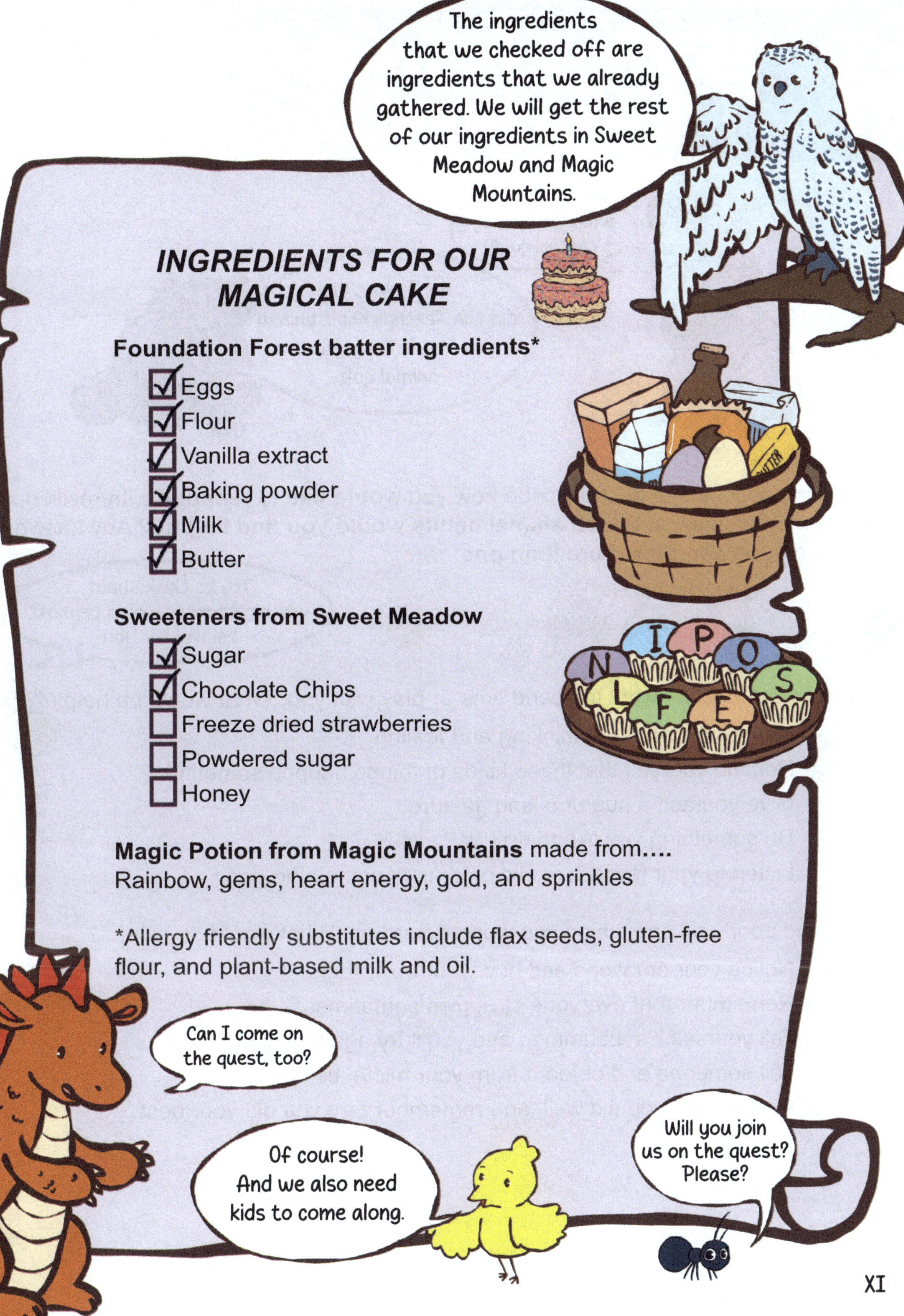

INGREDIENTS FOR OUR MAGICAL CAKE

Foundation Forest batter ingredients*

- [x] Eggs
- [x] Flour
- [x] Vanilla extract
- [x] Baking powder
- [x] Milk
- [x] Butter

Sweeteners from Sweet Meadow

- [x] Sugar
- [x] Chocolate Chips
- [ ] Freeze dried strawberries
- [ ] Powdered sugar
- [ ] Honey

Magic Potion from Magic Mountains made from....
Rainbow, gems, heart energy, gold, and sprinkles

*Allergy friendly substitutes include flax seeds, gluten-free flour, and plant-based milk and oil.

Quiz - What is your Resilence animal?

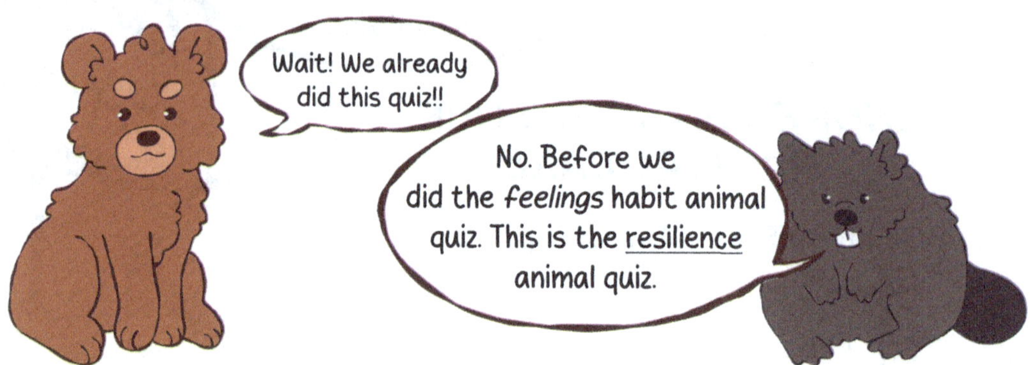

Circle the options that best describe how you **would like to respond** with resilience in the below situations. **Which animal habits would you find helpful?** Any answer is great, and **you can pick more than one.**

Try to think about which responses would be most helpful for you.

1. Your friend doesn't want to spend time or play with you. What would be helpful?
   -  Notice what you are thinking and feeling
   -  Remind yourself that these kinds of things happen sometimes
   -  Give yourself a hug or a kind gesture
   -  Do something you like to do
   -  Listen to your favorite music or think of something good

2. You did poorly on something you worked hard on. What would be helpful?
   -  Notice your emotions and how your body feels
   -  Remember that everyone struggles sometimes
   -  Tell yourself it's a bummer, and you'll try again next time
   -  Tell someone and/or learn from your mistakes
   -  Notice what you did well, and remember that you did your best

3. Someone close to you yells at you because you made a mistake. What would be helpful?

- Notice the stress in your body and take a few deep breaths
- Remember that everyone has difficult moments
- Tell yourself that it's going to be okay
- Shake off your stress
- Remind yourself that you're still a good person

4. If your friend was feeling sad, what would be helpful?

- Notice how your friend is feeling and how you feel, too
- Remind them they're not alone
- Ask them if they'd like a hug, or let them know you care
- Ask them if they'd like to play a game or hang out
- Try to make them smile

5. You feel upset and your friend or parent asks you what's wrong. What would be helpful?

- Tell them how you are feeling
- Ask them if they've ever felt like this
- Ask them for a hug or some understanding
- Ask them to do something with you
- After sharing why you're upset, thank them for listening

6. A friend or sibling is better than you at something you have been trying hard to improve. What would be helpful?

- Notice how you feel
- Remind yourself that it takes time to grow skills
- Be an understanding friend to yourself
- Practice the skill you'd like to improve
- Tell yourself you are still doing great

Giraffe	Dog	Bunny	Dolphin	Sun

Count up the number of different animals that you chose.

Below is a description of the animals you may have chosen. All of the responses can boost your resilience

If you had **mostly** , your resilience animal is SPOTS the giraffe. Do you like to notice your feelings, five senses, and body sensations? That's Spots' habit!

If you had **mostly** , your resilience animal is Buddy the dog. Do you like to remind yourself that other people sometimes feel like you? That's the Buddy habit!

If you had **mostly** , your resilience animal is Snuggles the bunny. Do you like to offer yourself comforting or encouraging words or kind touch when things go wrong? That's the Snuggles habit!

If you had **mostly** , your resilience animal is Doodles the dolphin. Do you like to take helpful actions like moving your body, playing a game, or solving problems? That's Doodles' habit!

If you had **mostly** , your resilience habit is Sunny. When things go wrong, do you remind yourself that good things are happening, too? That's the Sunny habit!

The more different responses and animals you have, the bigger your resilience toolkit will be. This is what an animal with all the resilience habits might look like.

Draw or write about your resilience animal (combination) below:

Don't worry if none of the animals feel like the right match yet. The more you practice, the more natural the resilience animal habits will become!

Meet the Kids' Team

You will go on this adventure with real kids who helped to create this book! These kids are also learning resilience habits.

Circle the kids who are growing the same resilience habit animals as you.

Resilience Habit Animals

 = Buddy - I'm not alone / It's okay to feel this way

 = Spots - Noticing your five senses, feelings, or thoughts

 = Sunny - Thinking of good things

 = Snuggles - Comforting or encouraging words or touch

 = Doodles - Actions that are kind to your body, mind or heart

Ambika: I like reading and playing tennis.

"When I get stressed, I like to think of common humanity (the Buddy habit), and I like to use mindfulness (Spots) like noticing my senses or how I feel."
-Ambika, age 12

Khalil: I like to play soccer and baseball. And I like to play video games.

"My resilience habit animal is Snuggles. I am kind to other people, and kindness comes back to me."
-Khalil, age 8

Anjali: I am creative with my sister, and I like acting and reading.

"I am mostly Snuggles the bunny and somewhat Doodles the dolphin (a dolphunny). And I'm trying to grow the Buddy and Sunny habits."
-Anjali, age 10

Dallas: I like to play soccer and look at my snakes.

Maya: I'm creative, and I like rollerblading and running. I also like Minecraft.

"I like to use the Buddy one–reminding myself I'm not alone, and the Doodles–I go for a run or I journal. And I'm getting more comfortable with the Snuggles one."
–Maya, age 14

All of the resilience animals are helpful.

River: I like exercising and eating healthy and playing games on my tablet.

Aarya: I am a big animal person, and I like to read and write.

Matteo: I like to play soccer and baseball, and I like to play video games.

Sofia: I enjoy reading and writing, as well as spending time with my pet rabbit.

"I'm a giraffe-bunny (Spots and Snuggles), but it doesn't feel natural yet."
–Sofia, age 14

Marcos: I like to play sports, and I like to win.

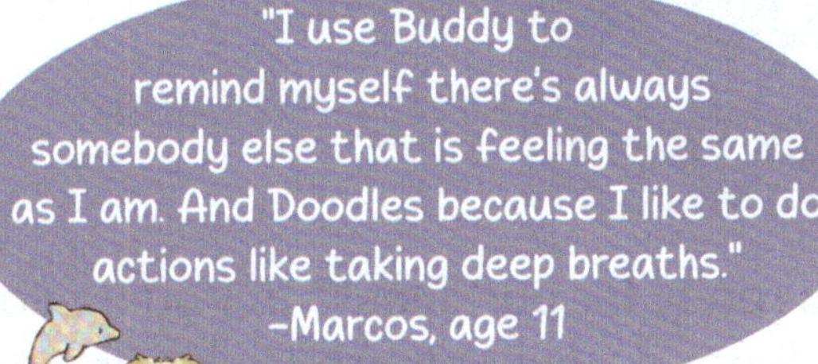

Abbie: I like being active. I like doing sports and am very happy around animals.

"I do the Doodles habit. I want to grow the Sunny and Snuggles habits, even though they are hard for me."
-Abbie, age 12

Color the outline how you'd like to look on this adventure. Feel free to be creative.

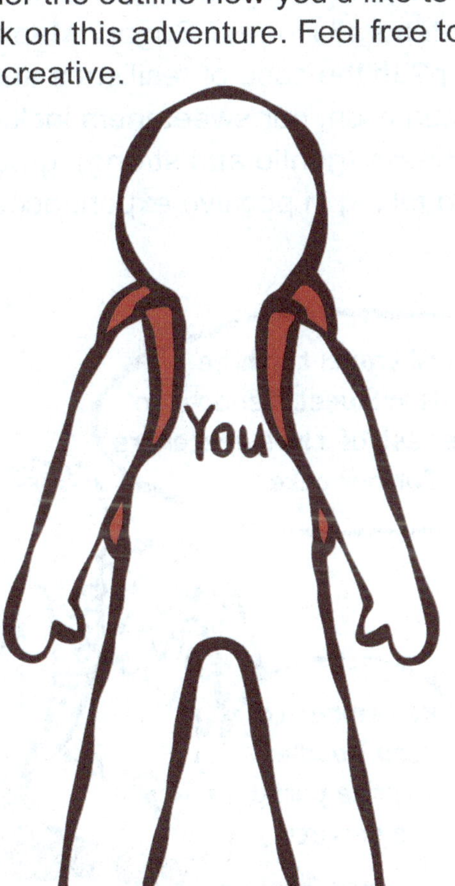

Write a quote about your resilience habit animals in the oval.

When you see this outline for "You" in our adventures, you can color it any way you wish.

Adventures in Sweet Meadow!

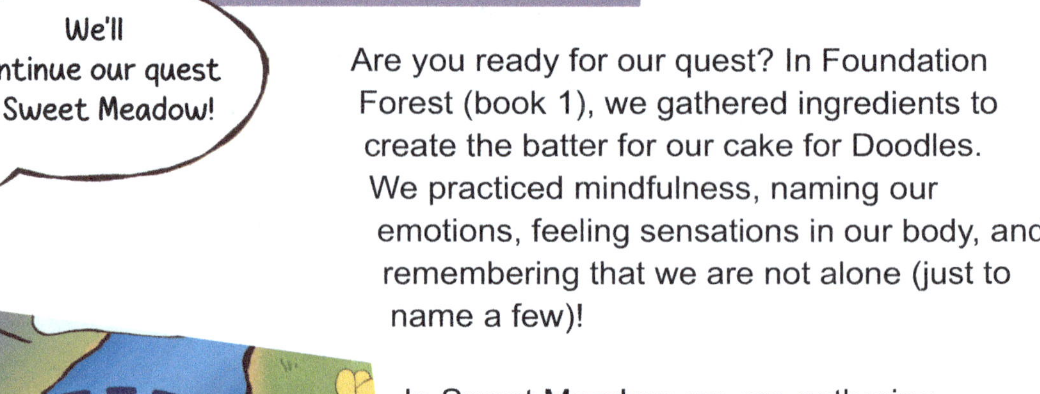

Are you ready for our quest? In Foundation Forest (book 1), we gathered ingredients to create the batter for our cake for Doodles. We practiced mindfulness, naming our emotions, feeling sensations in our body, and remembering that we are not alone (just to name a few)!

In Sweet Meadow, we are gathering sweeteners for our cake for Doodles' surprise party. What are your favorite sweeteners? Honey? Sugar? Maple syrup? In the case of resilience and self-compassion, our sweeteners include kindness (gentle and strong), gratitude, and taking in positive experiences.

Celebration

Comfort

Imagination

Sunshine

Sweet Meadow

We will travel to three more lands in Sweet Meadow to collect the rest of the sweeteners for our cake.

Remember to keep Doodles' surprise party a secret!

In our first adventure, we'll visit the Land of Sunshine.

MEET OUR FIRST COMIC CHARACTER, SAM

Sam likes to look at things logically and also loves building with legos. Sam has the chameleon feelings habit and is learning the SPOTS and Sunny habits.

Do you know what your feelings habit animal is? If not, take the quiz in the introduction to find out!

Hey! That's what I said in the first book!

I love these cookies!
COOKIES
They smell delicious!
Yeah I guess they do.
COOKIES
Do you want to take a deep breath and savor the yummy smell?
Sure...
mmmm...
Do you want to take a little bite and slowly notice the taste?
nod
You can do this with any good thing in life. When something makes you happy, you can slow down and really take it in.
COOKIES

Everyone has things they enjoy. What do you like to savor?

Join Anjali and Khalil for this adventure in the Land of Sunshine and grow your happiness! You'll get a sweetener for the magical cake when you complete this adventure!

TAKING IN THE GOOD

Have you ever had a really good day with one bad thing? When you got home, what did you think about? The one bad thing? Me too.

The memory part of our brain automatically notices and stores every challenging experience to try to avoid future problems. But our brain doesn't necessarily notice and remember the good things.

There are things we can do to help positive moments be more powerful in our minds. When something good happens, we can get curious about what we see, hear, smell, taste, and feel. Using our five senses can help us remember our up moments after they pass.

We can also slow down to savor good things. In the comic, Sam did this with food, but we can do this with other good moments, too.

No one can be happy all the time. But enjoying happy moments can help us balance out our down moments. We are being kind to ourselves when we notice and take in good things.

Whenever you see me with a pencil or a crayon, there is something to write or color.

Activity 1.1 Glitter Glue

Follow the steps below to learn how our brains respond to up moments (like favorite foods or fun games at recess) and down moments (like being bored or feeling left out).

- ☐ Step 1: Write a down moment in each box in the outline of the person.
- ☐ Step 2: Write an up moment in each box at the bottom of the page.
- ☐ Step 3: Cut or tear out the up moment squares so they are removed from the bottom of this page.
- ☐ Step 4: Place the up moment squares in the open spaces in the person's outline.
- ☐ Step 5: Pick up the workbook, and hold it so the person's outline is facing you.
- ☐ Step 6: Look at the next page after you finish steps 1-5.

Down Moment

Write your up moments below, but <u>don't</u> glue until *after* you do steps 3-6.

Down Moment

Cut or tear

Up Moment	Up Moment

Did you notice that the up moments didn't stick? This is what happens to our minds! The down moments stick, and the up moments slip away.

In order to help our up moments stick, we need to notice that we are having a good moment and then add a little glitter glue. We can apply glitter glue to our up moments by using our five senses and paying extra attention (maybe taking a few breaths). This can help us really soak in the goodness.

If you have some tape or glue (or better yet, glitter glue) make your up moments stick to the person's outline on the previous page.

Don't let your up moments slip away! Taking some deep breaths and noticing your five senses can help goodness "stick" in your mind.

Noticing good things is the Sunny Habit!

Activity 1.2 Five Finger Fun

Mindfulness and gratitude go hand-in-hand. We can help ourselves notice the moment and really take in good things.

All of the exercises are done best by tracing your hand with the opposite pointer finger. After you finish each exercise, write your feelings in the palm.

5 Finger Breathing - Trace your hand with your opposite pointer finger. Breathe in as you trace up to the fingertip, and breathe out as you trace back towards your hand.

5 Finger Gratitude - Trace your hand and think of one good thing for each finger. Then write how you feel below.

Write down one thing you sense on each finger.

Noticing your five senses is mindfulness!

5 Finger Senses - Each finger tip represents one of your five senses. Trace your first finger and notice one thing that you can see. For the second finger, notice one thing that you hear, etc.

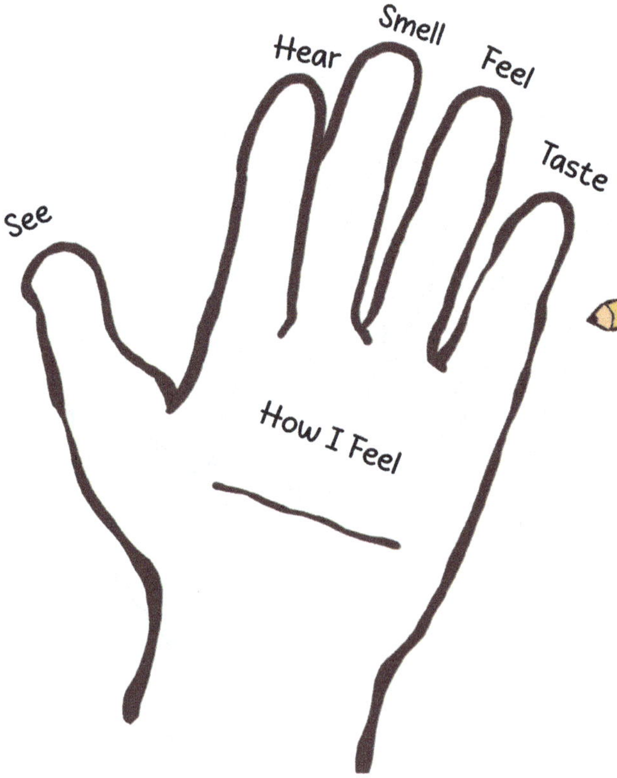

See
Hear
Smell
Feel
Taste
How I Feel

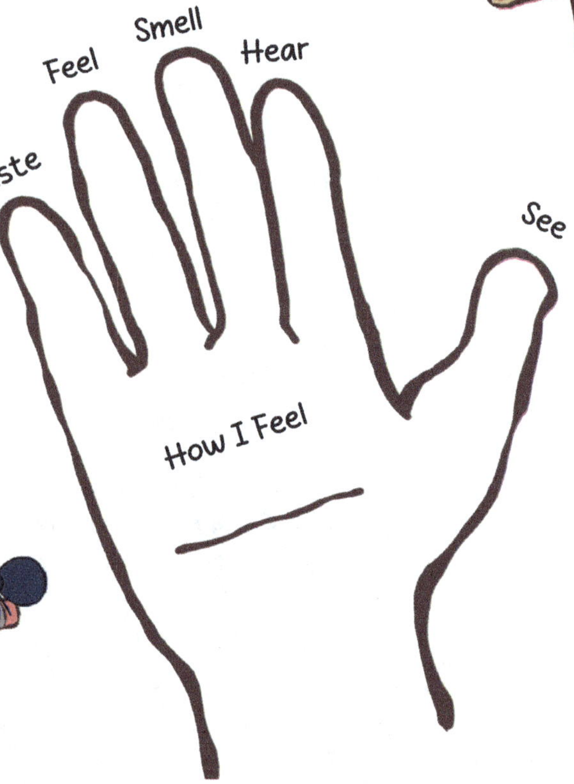

Taste
Feel
Smell
Hear
See
How I Feel

Gratitude for Your 5 Senses - Now mix gratitude with your senses. For your first finger, think of one thing you like to see (even if you can't see it right now). Then do this with hearing and your other senses.

Circle your favorite five finger exercise and think about when you might want to use it.

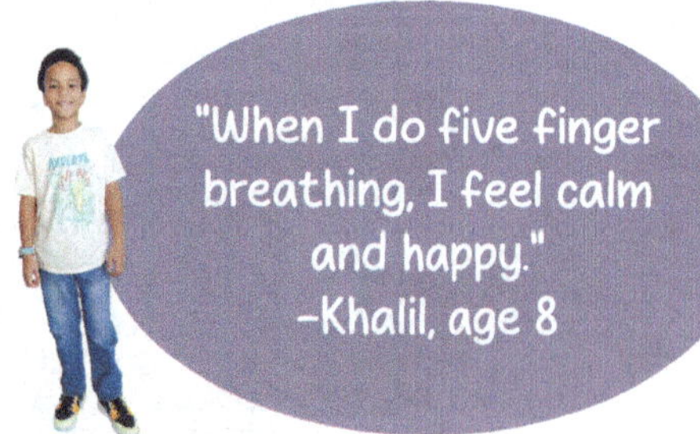

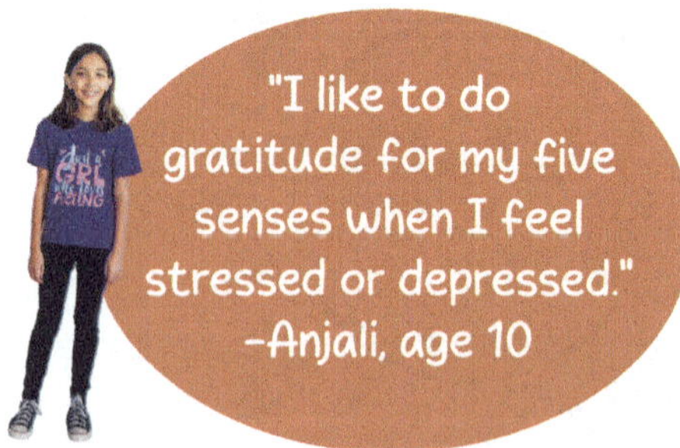

Activity 1.3 Life is a Rainbow

Life has good stuff and hard stuff. Good stuff and bad stuff don't cancel each other out. The good stuff is like the sun, and difficult stuff is like the rain. If we can notice the good stuff and also give ourselves kindness when life gets hard, a rainbow appears!

A note from Abbie:
I'm trying to grow the Sunny habit. At first I was trying to notice good things *instead* of bad things. Jamie Lynn taught me that trying to push away bad things and replace them with good things is actually hiding feelings (the chameleon habit). So now I'm trying to create space for difficult things AND good things. Sun and rain make a rainbow!

Abbie's rainbow example (something good and tricky at the same time):

My jeans are too tight and my shirt is comfy.

Your rainbow example (something good and tricky at the same time):

Activity 1.4 Cookie Breathing

What is your favorite kind of oven-baked cookie? Draw it below.

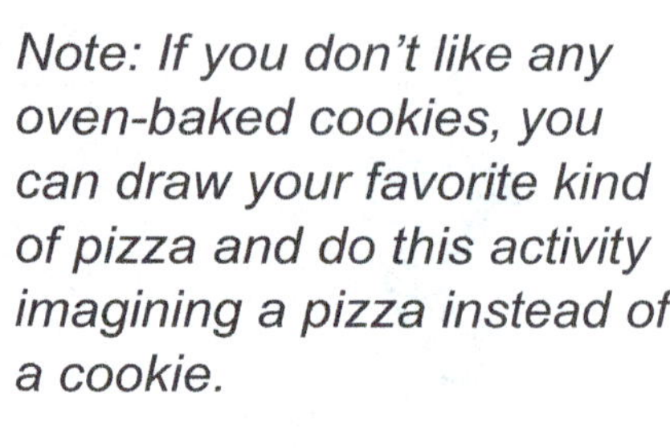

Note: If you don't like any oven-baked cookies, you can draw your favorite kind of pizza and do this activity imagining a pizza instead of a cookie.

Let's imagine that your favorite kind of cookie just came out of the oven. You are holding the cookie on a plate in front of you, but it is too hot to eat.

Take a deep breath in to savor the delicious, mouth watering smell. Mmmmmmm! Now blow on your cookie to cool it off.

It's still too hot to eat. Try this again.

Breathe in smelling your cookie....and breathe out to cool it down.

Oh, man! It's still a little too hot!! One more deep breath should do.

Breathe in and smell your cookie, and now breathe out all your breath.

Your cookie is finally ready to eat. Will you eat it fast or slow? ____________

You could do cookie breathing in daily life anytime. You can also practice "cookie breathing" to soak in positive experiences in life (like playing in the sprinkler on a hot summer day).

Adventure 1 Take-Aways

Resilience Habit Animals

 = Snuggles - Comforting or encouraging words or touch

 = Spots - Noticing your five senses, feelings, or thoughts

 = Sunny - Thinking of good things

You can circle your favorite ideas!

Ideas:

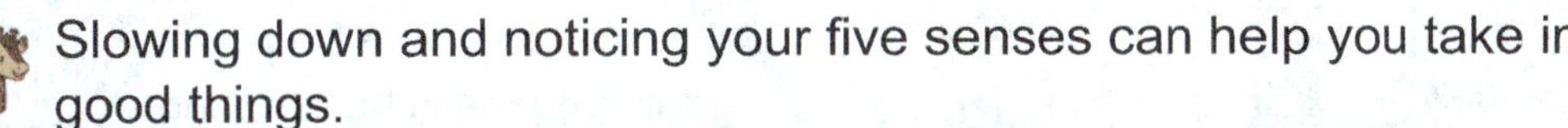

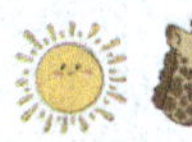 Slowing down and noticing your five senses can help you take in good things.

 Noticing good things (sun) and also noticing hard things with kindness (rain) can make a rainbow.

Helpful Practices:

  Five finger fun (5 finger breathing, gratitude, senses, or gratitude for your senses)

  Cookie Breathing

Bonus Activity:

Savoring Food: In the comic, Curi invited Sam to savor a cookie. You can do this with any food. Ask a grown-up to give you something you enjoy eating. Then use all of your senses as you eat it. Notice how the food looks, feels, smells, sounds, and tastes. Slow down and savor its yumminess.

Curiosity Question:

How does your body feel when you notice good things?

A Note for Grown-Ups:
Caring for kids can be both rewarding and hard. Make sure that you take time to soak in the good!

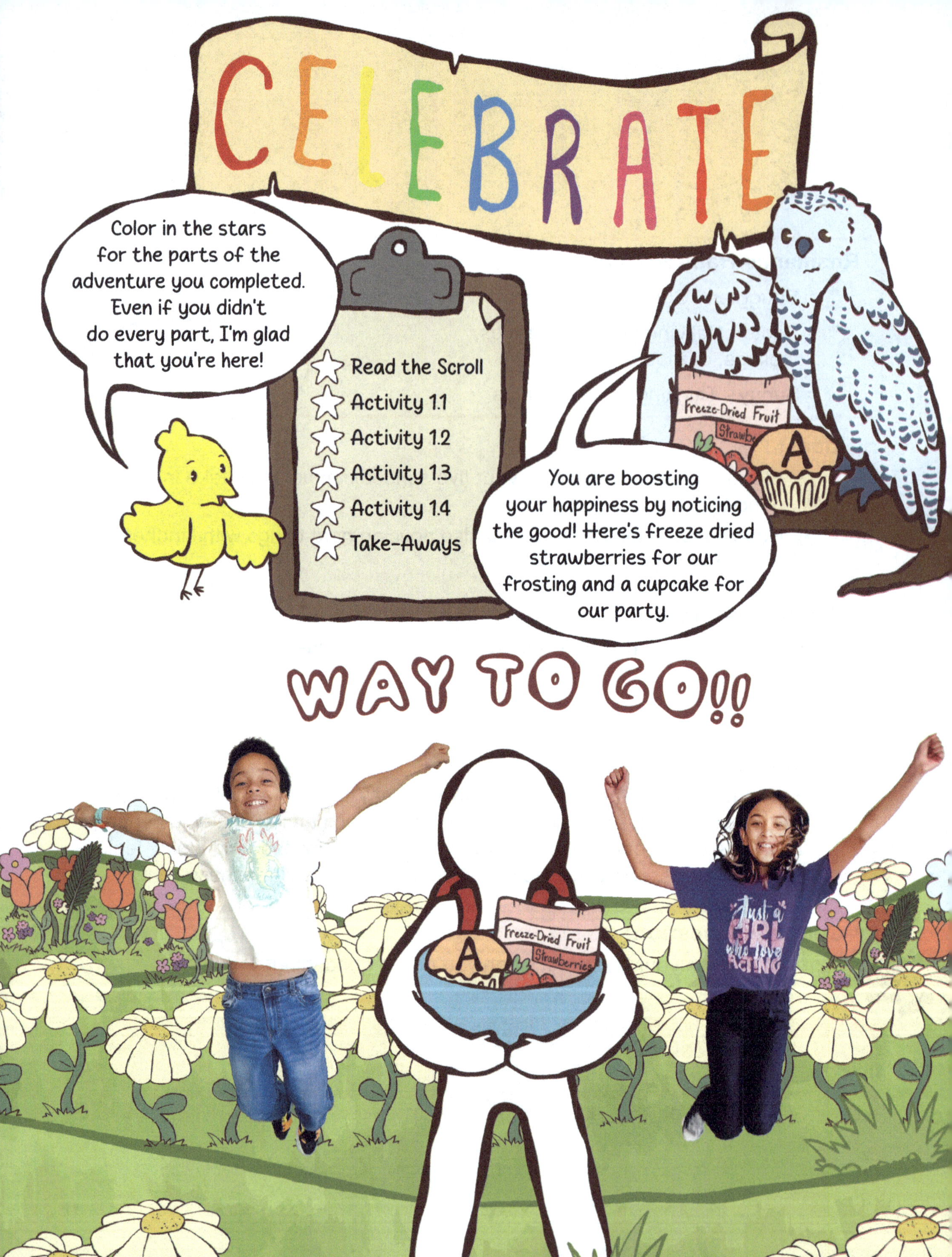
CELEBRATE
Color in the stars for the parts of the adventure you completed. Even if you didn't do every part, I'm glad that you're here!
Read the Scroll
Activity 1.1
Activity 1.2
Activity 1.3
Activity 1.4
Take-Aways
Freeze-Dried Fruit
A
You are boosting your happiness by noticing the good! Here's freeze dried strawberries for our frosting and a cupcake for our party.
WAY TO GO!!
A
Freeze-Dried Fruit
Strawberries

Chameleon is distracted at the park. Let's help Chameleon use Spots' and Sunny's habits and savor the moment.

In our next adventure, we'll visit the Land of Imagination

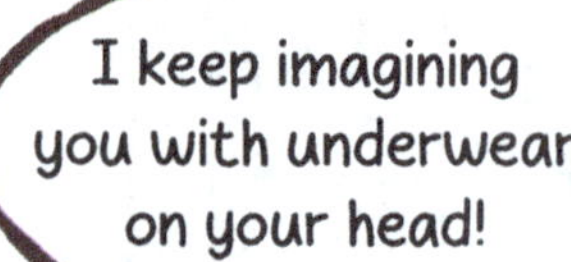

MEET OUR SECOND COMIC CHARACTER, ANITA

Anita is a kind friend. She sometimes worries that it's wrong to feel mad or sad. Anita likes to play piano but fears she is not good enough. Her feelings habit animals are a deer and a beaver, and she's growing all five of the resilience animal habits.

What if I fail my test?
It sounds like you're really worried. Did you study yet?
nod
Did you know that your brain worries because it wants you to be safe? It sees what could go wrong and can miss things that go well.
It might be helpful to notice ways you are okay right now, like how the sun is keeping you warm and gravity is hugging you to Earth.
We can help ourselves notice ways we are alright.

Everyone worries sometimes. What is something that you worry about?

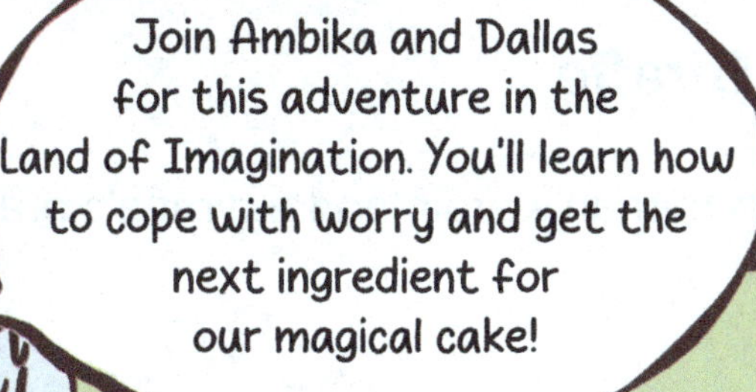

STICKY FOR THE TRICKY

Did you know that the human mind has grown over the years to focus on what could go wrong and try to avoid it!? This is because humans lived in the wild for a long, long time. We had to be alert for wild animals in order to stay alive. If we missed a predator in the bushes, we could become lunch!

Nowadays, our brain doesn't have to worry about being eaten by wild animals. Instead our brain worries about other things– like doing poorly on a test or wondering if our friends like us. It's not our fault that our brains worry, and there are things we can do to help.

If we are worried about something we need to do, we can take action! But when there is no action required, we can calm our minds.

We can name our worries. In the comic, Anita told Curi that she was worried about her test. We can also notice our five senses and remember we are not alone. Even though our brains can be sticky for the tricky, we can use resilience habits to help ourselves feel okay.

Activity 2.1 Imagine You're a Giraffe

Understanding the difference between a human's brain and a giraffe's brain can show us why the human mind can be tricky.

Imagine you are a giraffe in the wild.

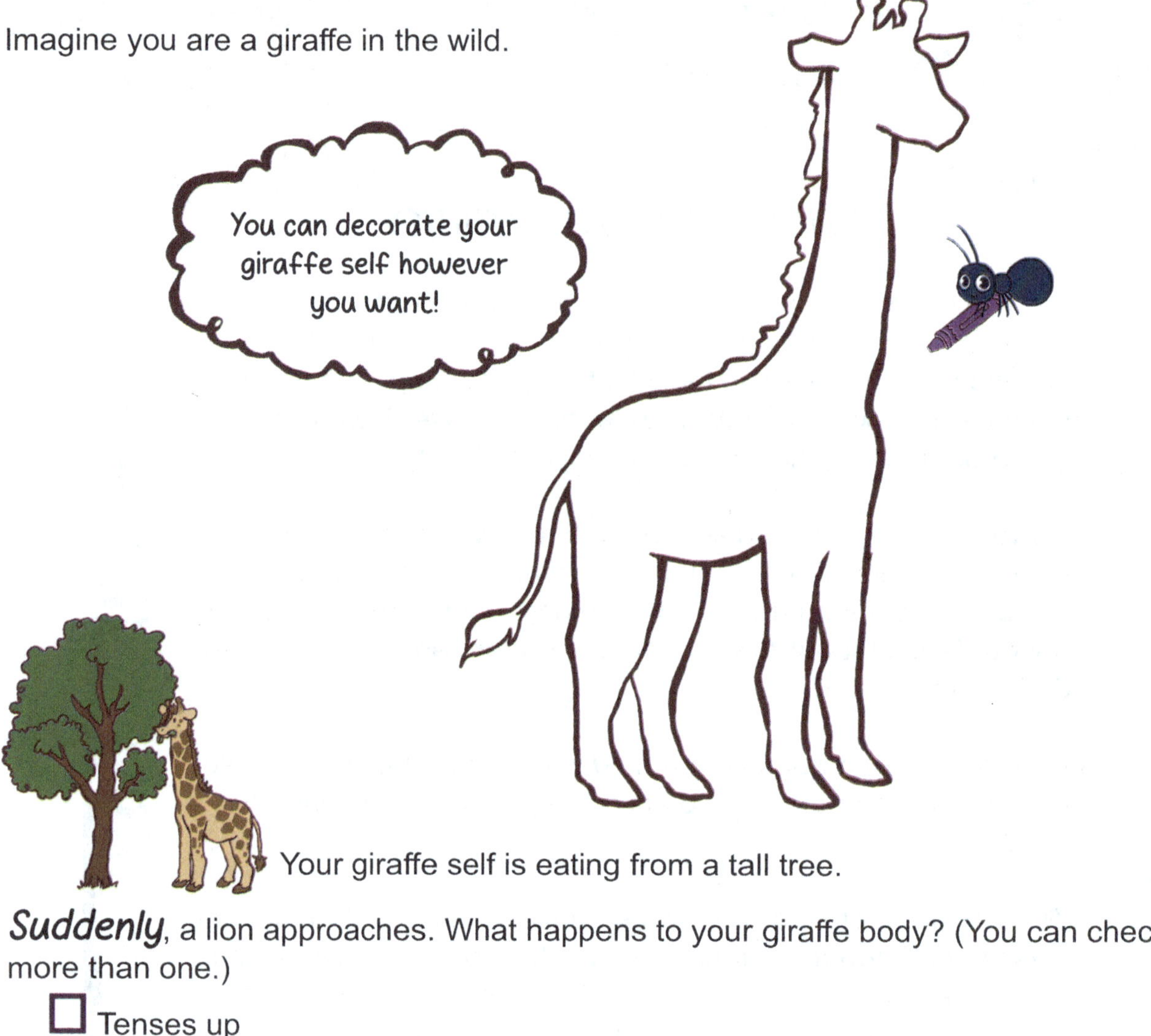

Your giraffe self is eating from a tall tree.

Suddenly, a lion approaches. What happens to your giraffe body? (You can check more than one.)

- ☐ Tenses up
- ☐ Heart starts beating fast
- ☐ Fight or Run away
- ☐ Freeze
- ☐ Other ____________

Now imagine that the lion is not very hungry, so the lion decides to go somewhere else.

What a relief!

If you were a giraffe, your body would calm down, and you would start eating again. Your brain would come back to the present moment. You would not be thinking about the lion. You would not be wondering if the lion would come again.

Now imagine if this happened to you as a human. What would you be thinking about after the lion went away?

____

____

A lot of kids (and grown-ups) say that they would remember the lion over and over, or worry, "What if the lion comes back again!?" A giraffe's brain returns to the present moment, but not a human brain.

In our daily life, we are not usually worried about lions eating us, so instead our brain worries about other things.

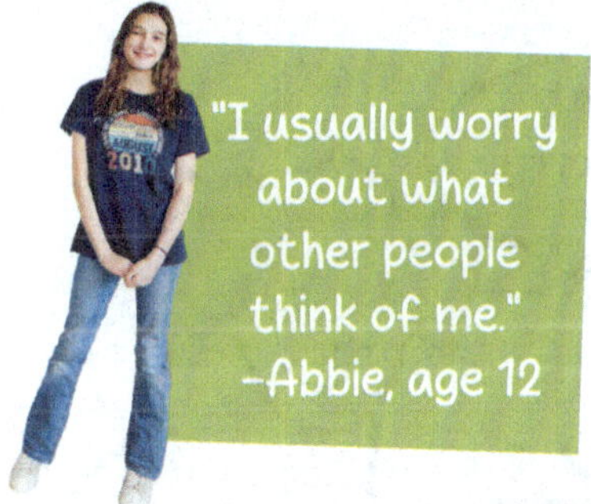

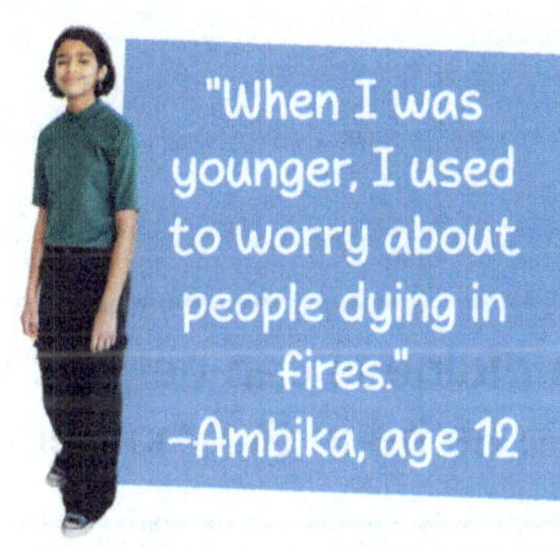

What does your mind worry about?

____

____

Let's help our mind come back to the present moment. You can do your favorite five finger breathing practice from pages 8-9.

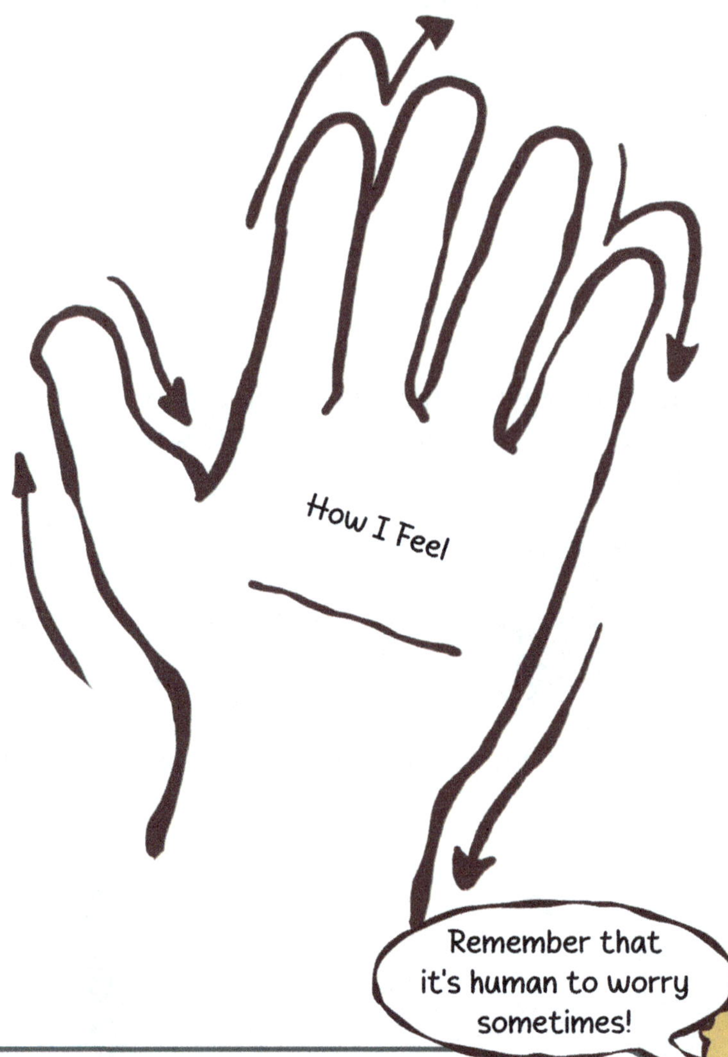

Remember that it's human to worry sometimes!

Mindfulness can help us to deal with our worries. It can help us be in the moment like a giraffe.

A Note for Grown-Ups:

If your child struggles with worry, your child may benefit from the foundational skills taught in Volume 1 of this workbook. We need to learn and practice mindfulness skills in low stress situations before we can apply them to worry.

Activity 2.2 Connecting our Brain

When our brain starts to worry, sometimes it can feel like a thunderstorm or a tornado takes over our mind. Understanding what's happening in our brain, and how to best respond can help us find shelter as we wait for the storm to pass.

There are two parts of our brain that are helpful to know about: the alarm (amygdala) and the wise part of our brain (the prefrontal cortex or PFC).

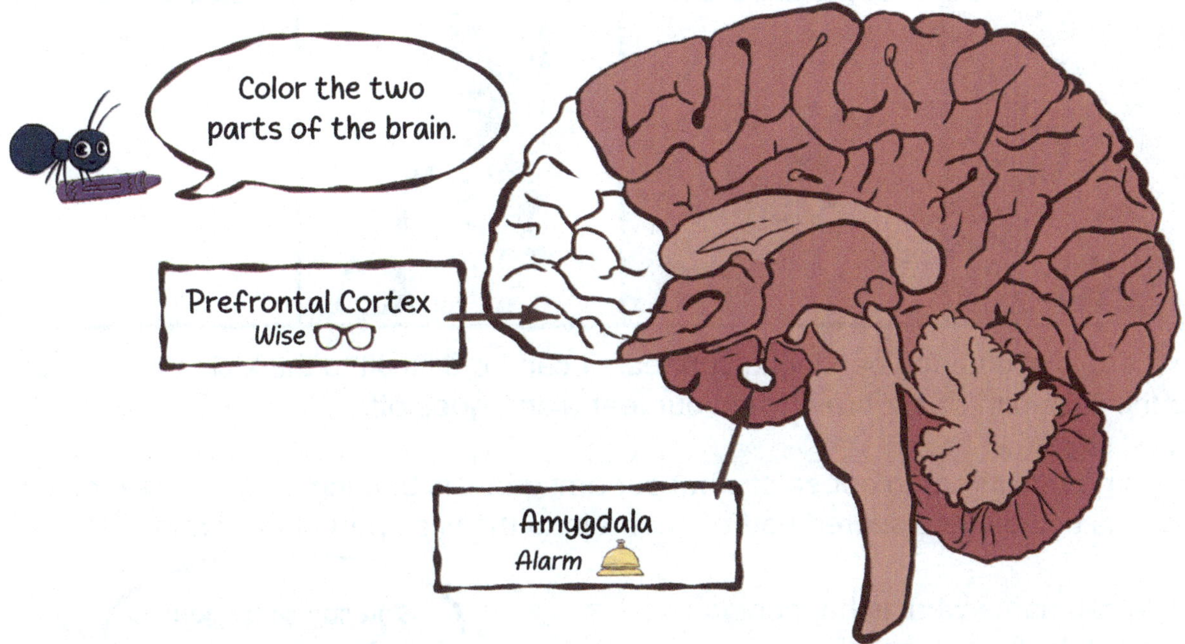

The amygdala is the fear part of our brain. It's designed to protect us. In the giraffe exercise we just did, the giraffe's amygdala sounded its alarm when the lion approached. **With a real threat, our fear (amygdala's) alarm is helpful**.

Unfortunately, our fear alarm is not always good at figuring out which threats are real. When we have a scary thought or a big emotion, our brain might view our thoughts and feelings as real threats, even though we are actually safe in the moment. Maybe we feel afraid that someone doesn't like us or that we're not good at something. Our brain says, "Oh no! This is not okay!" and our amygdala sounds the alarm.

This kind of alarm is like a small dog looking out the front window of a house and barking very loudly at everything that passes by. The loud, barking dog thinks that everything it sees outside the window is a threat, but the dog is actually safe inside the house.

Circle or draw your little, scared dog (your amygdala with a false alarm).

			other:

When there is a loud dog barking in your ear, it can be difficult to think clearly. It's hard to use the wise part of our brain when our fear alarm goes off.

If there is no real threat to our safety, but our amygdala is barking loudly, these things can help us connect the scared part of our brain to the wise part of our brain.

You can circle your favorite ideas!

 We can name what is happening (speak to the dog calmly).

 We can notice our five senses, including sights and sounds and the bottoms of our feet (help the dog look around).

 We can move our bodies. Exercising, stretching, or slowing down our breathing can help (take the dog for a walk).

 We can offer ourselves kindness and remember that everyone feels this way sometimes (pet the dog).

A trusted grown-up can help you identify real threats to your safety and give you the support you need. Grown-ups can also help you deal with worries that are "false alarms" (like a monster under your bed).

Activity 2.3 Resilience Habits for Worry

You can try these ideas the next time you feel worried. They won't make your fear magically go away, but they can definitely help!

Activity 2.4 Compassionate Friend

Our imagination is very powerful. Even though we sometimes imagine tricky things, we can also use our imagination to help us feel safe and loved.

We are going to do an imaginative exercise and imagine ourselves in a safe, relaxing place. What peaceful place would you like to imagine? It could be a place in nature, like by a pond or a forest. It could also be a cozy spot in your house or a friend's home. It could even be an imaginary place, like floating on clouds.

Draw or describe your peaceful place here.

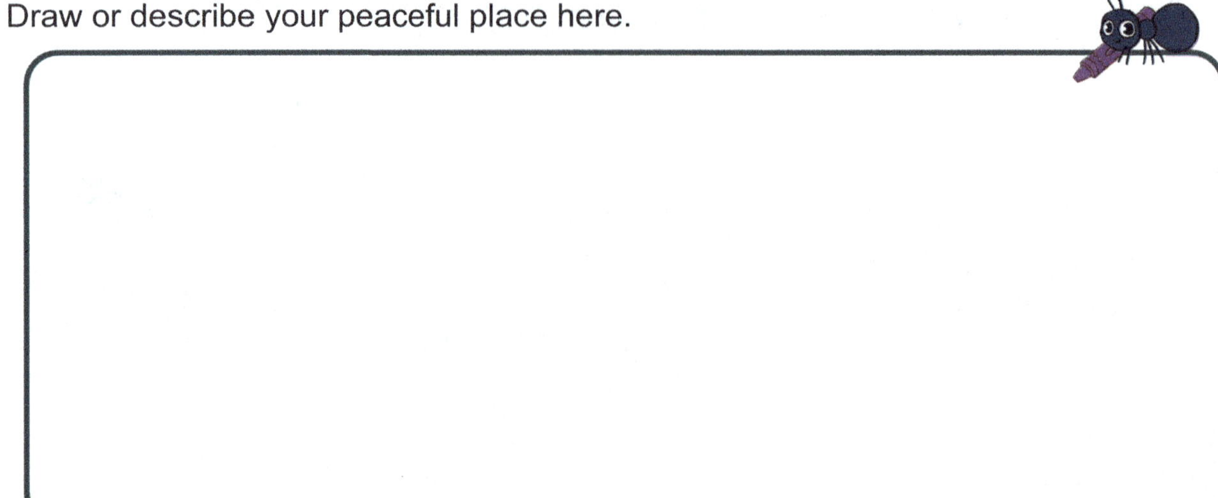

In our imagination exercise, a kind and compassionate friend will visit us. When you imagine your friend, you can imagine anyone you want. Your kind friend could be....

- A family member or a friend
- A pet
- A superhero
- An imaginary creature, like a kitty with wings
- It could be ANYTHING!

Someone who is going to be there....just for you.

You can do the Compassionate Friend on your own, or you can ask an adult to read it to you or help you listen to an audio recording at: https://jamielynntatera.com/workbook-for-kids-guided-practices/

If you are listening, you can either relax and imagine, or you can draw your compassionate friend while you listen.

A Note for Grown-Ups:
If you read this exercise to your child, be sure to pause to allow time for imagining.

Compassionate Friend Guided Visualization

To begin, you can imagine that you are in your safe and peaceful place. Notice what you see, smell, hear, and sense. Savor how it feels to be in this place.

Our compassionate friend will visit us soon. This friend could be a real person or an animal or even a warm light. Let's imagine our friend now. What do they look like, and how does it feel when you are with them?

You have a choice. You can leave your peaceful place and go out to meet your friend, or you can invite them in. You may do this now.

Imagine you and your friend together—feeling comfortable, safe, happy and loved. Your compassionate friend knows you well and cares about you so much. They might have something to say to you. Go ahead and listen to what they have to say—words that you like to hear.

And if they don't say anything, that's ok. Maybe you are just enjoying being with them.

Maybe there is something that you want to say to your compassionate friend. They are a very good listener. Go ahead and say anything you'd like to say to your friend.

Let yourself take some time to soak in the goodness of being with your friend.

You are able to imagine kind things because this kindness is inside of you. Notice how you feel when you realize that kindness and compassion are a part of you. You can call on your compassionate friend any time you wish.

Now you can let this image slowly melt away in your mind and come back to yourself in this room. Wiggle your toes, and feel the sensations in your body. If you closed your eyes, you can open them.

**This guided practice is used in the Self-Compassion for Children and Caregivers program and has been adapted from Paul Gilbert's Compassionate Image meditation.*

Draw or write about your compassionate friend in the box below.

A Note for Grown-Ups:
The Compassionate Friend exercise can be a great way for kids to begin to offer themselves compassion. When they are struggling, they can imagine their Compassionate Friend (a friend, dog, bunny, etc.) offering them kind words. This becomes a bridge for kids to eventually offer this kindness to themselves.

Adventure 2 Take-Aways

Resilience Habit Animals

 = Buddy - I'm not alone / It's okay to feel this way

 = Spots - Noticing your five senses, feelings, or thoughts

 = Sunny - Thinking of good things

 = Snuggles - Comforting or encouraging words or touch

 = Doodles - Actions that are kind to your body, mind or heart

Ideas:

 Our mind can be sticky for the tricky, and it's not our fault.

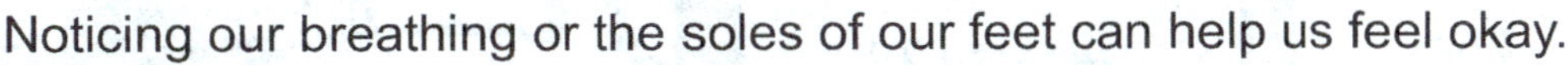 Noticing our breathing or the soles of our feet can help us feel okay.

 Resilience habits can help when we feel stressed.

Helpful Practices:

 Notice and name when your brain's worry alarm goes off

When it's a false alarm, and your dog starts barking, you can:

 Pet the dog (kindness).

 Talk to the dog in a soothing voice (name what is happening).

 Take the dog for a walk (move your body).

Or help the dog focus on something else (notice your five senses).

 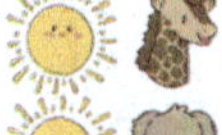 Remember the helpful habit animals when you feel worried

 Compassionate Friend Imagination Exercise

Bonus Activity:

Name your dog from Activity 2.2: Get a good picture of your small, scared dog in your mind, and give it a nickname. When your amygdala starts to worry unnecessarily, you can picture your dog and call it by its nickname. (You could also picture your dog with underwear on its head!) Then figure out how to best respond to your dog.

Curiosity Question:

Who can you talk to about your worries?

A Note for Grown-Ups:
It can be very difficult for kids (and grown-ups) to use helpful strategies when the amygdala sounds the alarm. That's why it's important to help kids practice mindfulness and kindness when they are feeling okay.

CELEBRATE
I'm happy that you're learning so much!
Read the Scroll
Activity 2.1
Activity 2.2
Activity 2.3
Activity 2.4
Take-Aways
We're using our imagination in helpful ways! Here's powdered sugar for our magical cake and a cupcake for our party.
YOU'RE A RESILIENCE SUPER STAR!

Beaver is worrying about striking out. Let's help Beaver use Spots' and Snuggles' helpful habits.

In our next adventure, we'll visit the Land of Comfort.

This is our last adventure in Sweet Meadow. We have almost all the sweeteners for Doodles' cake!

Comfort

We all need comfort when things don't go our way.

Nothing comforts me when I'm upset!!

MEET OUR THIRD COMIC CHARACTER, JAMES

James is a big basketball fan. James gets really excited when he is looking forward to something, and he gets really mad or sad when things don't work out. James' feelings habit animal is a bear. He is growing the Snuggles and Buddy habits.

Why does Jake have to move away! I'll never be happy again!
MOVING
I'm sorry that your friend is moving. Would you like a hug?
How can you give me a hug? Your wings are so small!
What if you gave yourself a hug?
I would feel a little silly if I hugged myself, but I'll try it.
I am here for you. And you can also be there for yourself.

There are lots of different ways that kids comfort themselves. How do you like to comfort yourself when you're upset?

COMFORT IN ACTION

When you are upset, do you like to receive a hug from a friend or a trusted grown-up? Just like words can comfort a person, so can touch.

In the comic, James learned he could offer a hug to himself. Comforting gestures can calm our bodies and minds. Some comforting gestures include a self-hug, resting your face in your hands, or tracing circles on your palm.

Sometimes just noticing your sense of touch can help to calm your mind. You might enjoy petting a pet, holding a stuffed animal, or playing with a fidget toy.

Kind touch is not the only way to help ourselves with tricky situations. We can offer ourselves kind words and take kind actions. When things go wrong, sometimes coloring, reading, or going outside can be self-compassionate. We can take actions that are kind to our body, mind, and heart.

Activity 3.1 Mindful Hands

Rub your hands together. What do they feel like? (You can check more than one.)

- ☐ Moist
- ☐ Warm
- ☐ Other ______________________________

Clap your hands together three times. What sensations do you notice?

- ☐ Prickly
- ☐ Tingly
- ☐ Other ______________________________

Trace your hand or fingers in this box. Notice what you feel when the pencil touches your skin. After you trace your fingers, write the sensations you can feel (warm, tingly, cold, ticklish, etc.).

Different Ways to Explore: Every body is different. You can do the activities on this page and the next with any body parts that work for you.

Noticing the sensations of our hands and body can focus and soothe our mind.

Notice sensations that you feel when you touch different objects. Below are some examples. You can try objects from different categories, and check your favorites.

- ☐ Feel the ground, the cover of this book, or a pencil.
- ☐ Squeeze a stuffed animal, pet a pet, snuggle in a blanket, or feel your clothing.
- ☐ Play with a fidget toy or slime.
- ☐ Rub something natural, like a rock, a leaf, or a stick.

Try touching different objects and notice how they feel.

What textures and temperature is most fun to feel (smooth, rough, soft, warm, cool, etc.)?

____

____

"I like touching my stuffies because they are soft, and my iPad because it is smooth."
-Dallas, age 7

Throughout the day, you can notice your sense of touch. That's part of the Spots habit!

Activity 3.2 Comforting Gestures

In the comic, James comforted himself with a hug because he was sad. We can offer ourselves touch as a way to soothe ourselves when we are feeling stressed. Find out what sorts of gestures feel most comforting to you.

You can try out the actions below and circle ALL of your favorites.

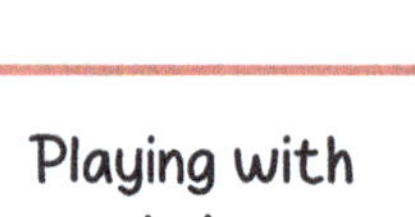

Playing with hair

Pointer fingers touching

Rubbing arms

Hands on cheeks

Rocking body

Hands on belly

Self-hug

Hands on heart

One hand on belly and the other hand on heart

Hugging thumb

Other idea ______________

I like my left hand on top, and my right hand on my belly. But I actually like both hands on my belly even better.
–Aarya, age 10

You can try your favorite gesture when you're having hard time.

What gesture did you like the best?

_ _

Activity 3.3 Monsters Under the Bed

Do you ever feel like your feelings are like monsters?

- ☐ Yes
- ☐ No

You can write or draw about monster feelings.

Difficult feelings and monsters are alike. Even though monsters are not real, we might still feel scared. Monsters and difficult feelings can seem scary, but they are not really something to be afraid of.

Flame's feelings were hiding under the bed. Hiding feelings for a long time can make us feel worse.

In the story below, Anjali, from the Kids Team, talks about her habit of hiding feelings, and how self-compassion helps.

"At school, sometimes my feelings get hurt, and I hide my feelings. Other times I get really mad at someone, but I don't tell anyone about it.

At home, when me and my sister get into fights, sometimes I pretend I don't care. And when I hide a lot of feelings and something tiny happens, sometimes all of my feelings explode out.

When I give myself compassion, it helps my feelings come out of hiding nicely, and then they can become my friends."

Can you think of a time when you or someone else hid feelings?

_ _

_ _

Our feelings do not seem scary once we know how to be with them.

Decode the message below to find out the best way to practice self-compassion when you have a lot of hidden feelings.

○	▽	□	☆	✦	♥
T	B	Y	I	E	L

L _ _ _ _ _   _ _   _ _ _ _ _ _

♥ ☆ ○ ○ ♥ ✦   ▽ □   ♥ ☆ ○ ○ ♥ ✦

I'm glad I get to do this a little at a time.

In Magic Mountains, we'll grow more self-compassion, which can really help!

Activity 3.4 Kind Actions

In addition to offering ourselves kind words and kind touch, we can also take kind actions. We can take actions to be kind to our minds, bodies, and hearts.

In the below picture, color the kind action by its category (mind, body, or heart).

- Color **blue** the actions that are **kind to your mind**.
- Color **brown** the actions that are **kind to your body**.
- Color **green** the actions that are **kind to your heart**.

Many actions may fit into more than one category, so don't worry if the colors get a little mixed up!

What kind actions do you like to do?

____

____

Taking action can help a lot when things go wrong.

"I like to rest, take deep breaths, and exercise." -Khalil, age 8

"When I'm stressed, I like to take care of my plants." -Sofia, age 14

Kind actions are great to do anytime! When things go wrong, taking a kind action can be an act of self-compassion.

Adventure 3 Take-Aways

Resilience Habit Animal

 = Spots - Noticing your five senses, feelings, or thoughts

 = Snuggles - Comforting or encouraging words or touch

 = Doodles - Actions that are kind to your body, mind or heart

You can circle your favorite ideas!

Ideas:

  When we are struggling, we can notice the touch of our hands or offer ourselves kind touch.

 We can practice self-compassion little-by-little.

 Actions are kind to ourselves if they are good for us both now and later.

Helpful Practices:

 Notice your sense of touch.

 Offer yourself a comforting gesture when things go wrong.

 Practice kind actions.

Bonus Activity:

Make a poster of kind actions that you could take when you are upset. Be sure to include actions that are kind to your mind, body, and heart.

Curiosity Question:

Do you prefer kind words, comforting gestures, or kind actions (or all three)?

A Note for Grown-Ups:

It takes a while for some kids to open to the idea of self-soothing. Often kids prefer to receive compassion from others. When a child is upset, it's helpful to first offer the child a supportive response, and then, if the child seems open, you can invite the child to offer compassion to themselves. Your supportive response and/or modeling of self-compassion will help the child develop self-compassion over time.

CELEBRATE
We've finished our adventures in Sweet Meadow!
Read the Scroll
Activity 3.1
Activity 3.2
Activity 3.3
Activity 3.4
Take-Aways
It's great that you're learning about what comforts you. Here's honey for our magical cake, and a cupcake for our surprise party!
Honey
WE'VE FINISHED SWEET MEADOW!
M
Honey
Yum! I love honey!

Bear is jealous of Little Sister Bear. Let's help Bear use Snuggles' and Doodles' helpful habits.

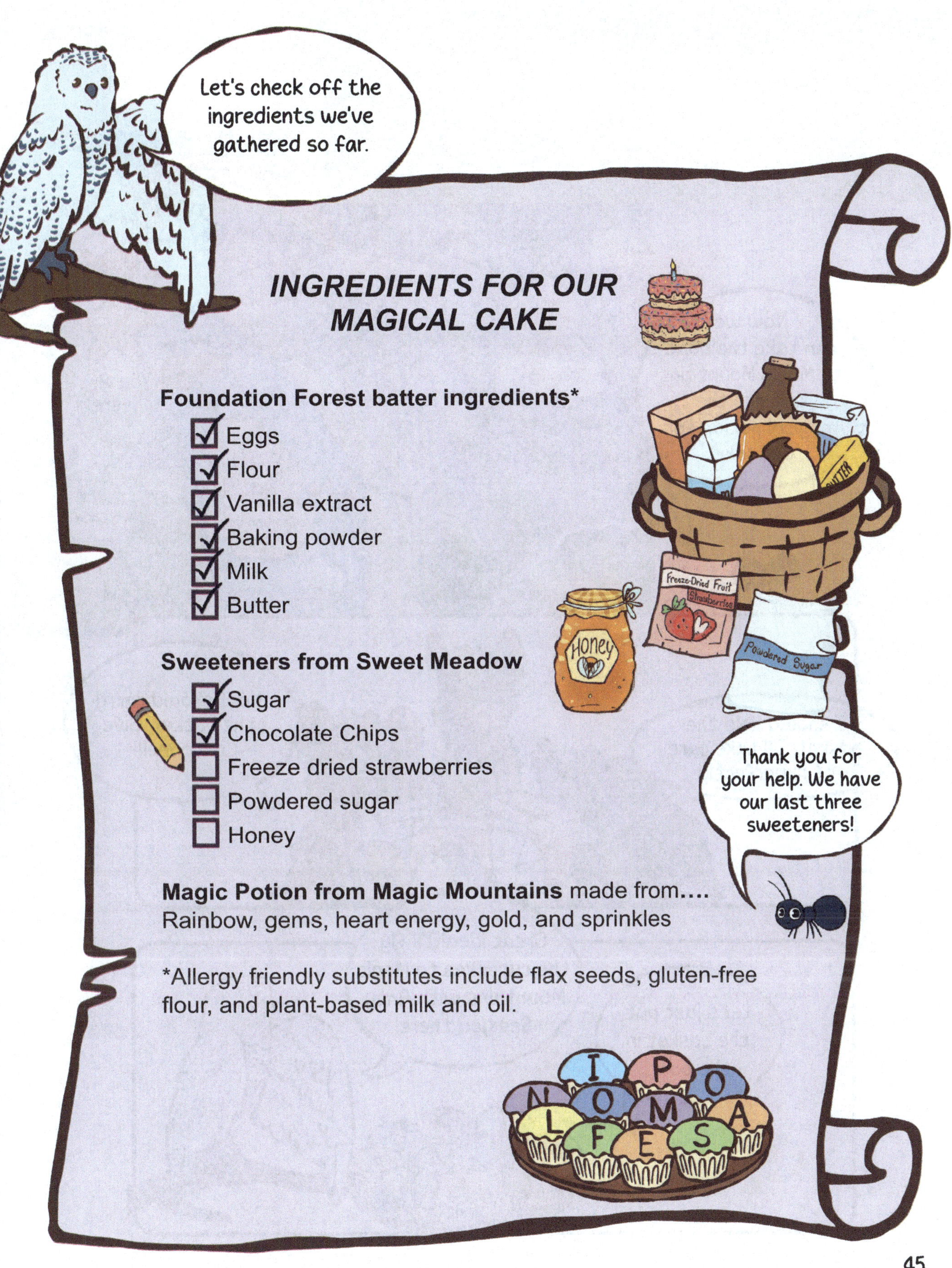

INGREDIENTS FOR OUR MAGICAL CAKE

Foundation Forest batter ingredients*

- [x] Eggs
- [x] Flour
- [x] Vanilla extract
- [x] Baking powder
- [x] Milk
- [x] Butter

Sweeteners from Sweet Meadow

- [x] Sugar
- [x] Chocolate Chips
- [ ] Freeze dried strawberries
- [ ] Powdered sugar
- [ ] Honey

Magic Potion from Magic Mountains made from....
Rainbow, gems, heart energy, gold, and sprinkles

*Allergy friendly substitutes include flax seeds, gluten-free flour, and plant-based milk and oil.

Congratulations! You've finished all of the adventures in Sweet Meadow!!

Adventures in Magic Mountains!

We now have almost all of the ingredients for Doodles' magical cake!

In Sweet Meadow we added sweeteners to our basic ingredients, including kind touch, words, and actions. These ingredients make difficult moments more sweet!

In Magic Mountains we will be adding magical ingredients and baking our dessert. We will "bake" our self-compassion skills by practicing them in challenging situations: when we are angry, when we fall short, and when we need encouragement.

Now on to Magic Mountains for our next adventure!

In our first adventure in Magic Mountains, we'll visit the Land of Self-Compassion.

I feel like I worry a lot.
That's hard.
Noticing your worries is the first step in dealing with them. Does talking to me help?
Yeah, but I still wish my mind didn't worry so much.
There are other kids who worry a lot, too.
Can you give yourself a little hug and remind yourself that you're okay?
Is there something you would like to do? We can't make difficult feelings go away, but we can be kind to ourselves while we wait for them to pass.
Let's go outside.

Everyone struggles sometimes. What is something you have a hard time with?
Anita has a hard time with worrying.
I struggle with accepting that I can't fly.
I struggle with being a perfectionist. -River, age 9
I have a hard time finishing my homework on time. -Aarya, age 10
You
You are entering the Land of Self-Compassion

GIVING KINDNESS TO OURSELVES

Can you think of a time when you gave or received kindness? Maybe someone smiled at you or opened a door for you. Or maybe *you* opened a door for someone else. Kindness is like the sun–it warms us up!

We can practice kindness at any time–including being kind to ourselves! Offering ourselves kind wishes or celebrating when we reach a goal are types of self-kindness.

Giving ourselves kindness when we struggle is self-compassion. Our struggle is like the rain, and kindness is like the sun. Putting these two things together can make a rainbow of self-compassion.

Self-compassion has three parts. In the comic, Anita noticed that her mind was worrying, so she named it. Noticing our struggles is the first part of self-compassion. Curi then helped her to remember that all kids worry sometimes. Remembering we are not alone is the second part. Finally, Curi invited Anita to be kind to herself, which is the third part of self-compassion. Kindness can include words, touch or actions.

When we mix these three parts together, we have a powerful recipe for self-compassion that can help us when things go wrong.

Activity 4.1 Kindness and Compassion

Kindness can be given, observed, and received. It can be big or small, like sharing a treat or telling a classmate, "Good job!"

Draw or write about an act of kindness that you have seen, given, or received.

When we are kind because someone is struggling, our kindness becomes compassion.

For example, if you give a flower to someone, it is an act of kindness. But if you give them flowers because they are sad or sick, it is an act of compassion.

We can also give kindness and compassion to ourselves. Taking care of our bodies by eating healthy food or getting good sleep is self-kindness. If we do these same things because we feel stressed, it is self-compassion.

 **SELF-kindness when YOU are**  **struggling → SELF-compassion**

The pictures are clues.

Write the following words in the crossword puzzle using the clues.

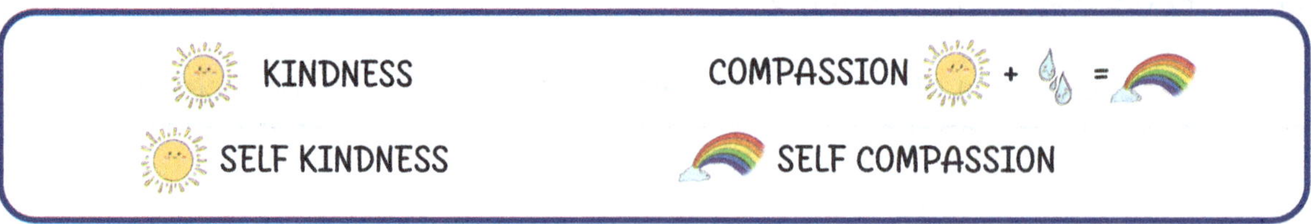

1. Giving your**self** a hug when things go wrong.
2. Smiling at a friend in school.
3. Congratulating your**self** for reaching a goal.
4. Including someone who is feeling left out in a game you are playing.

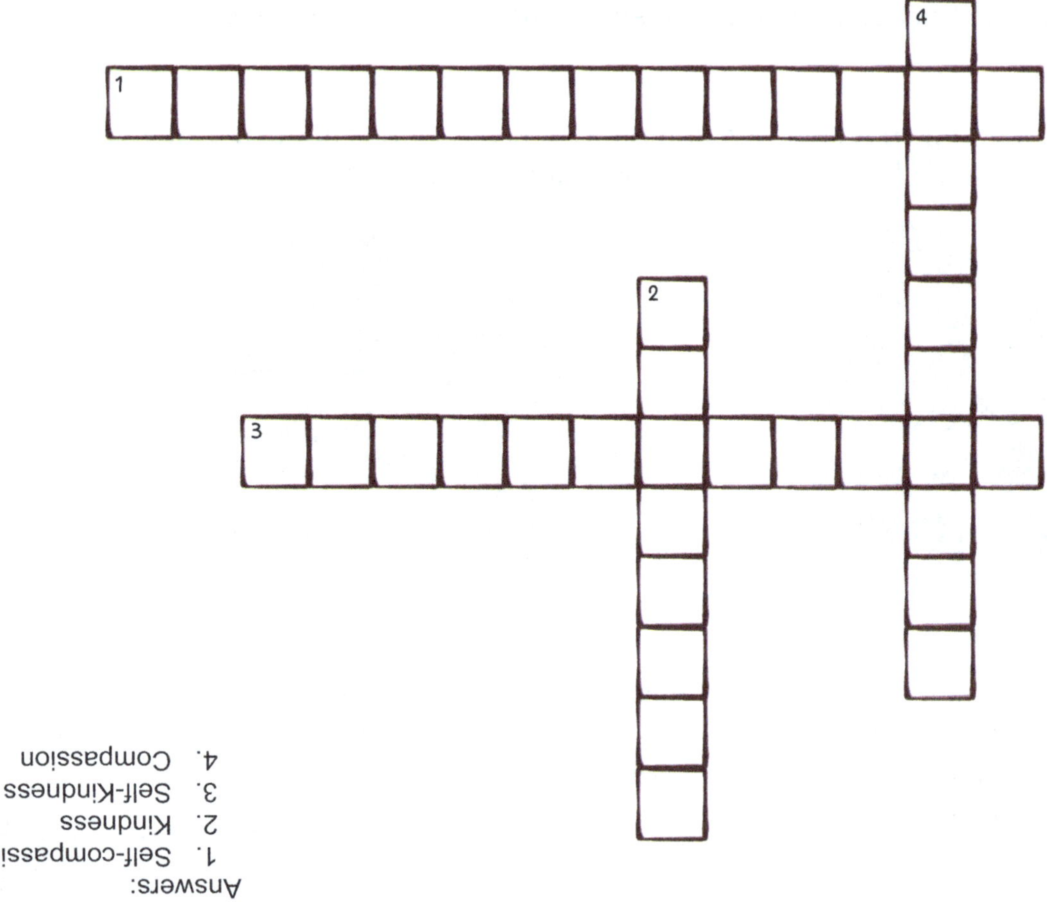

Answers:
1. Self-compassion
2. Kindness
3. Self-Kindness
4. Compassion

Don't worry if these definitions are a little confusing. Kindness, compassion, self-kindness, and self-compassion are all good things!

Activity 4.2 The Three Parts

Imagine you are walking down the sidewalk, and you hear a noise. You look down and see a little bird on the ground, shaking. Then you look up and see a nest of birds in the tree above you.

I would want to help. I know what it's like to not be able to fly.

How do you feel as you look at the small bird shaking on the ground? A little sad? Caring? Do you wish to help? Do you help it?

____

If so, you are feeling compassion. Noticing the struggling bird, feeling a connection, and wishing to help it are the three parts of compassion. If you actually helped the bird, that is part of compassion, too.

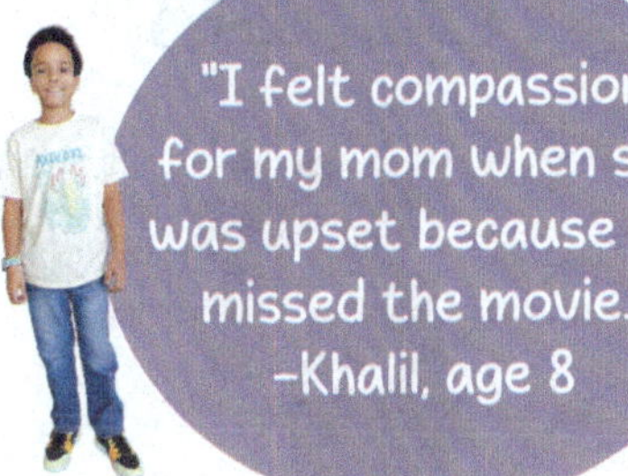

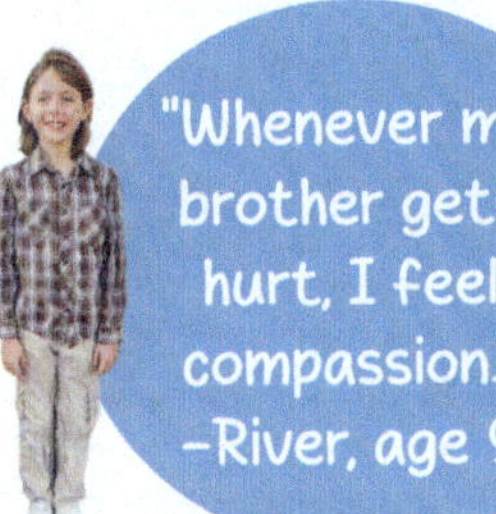

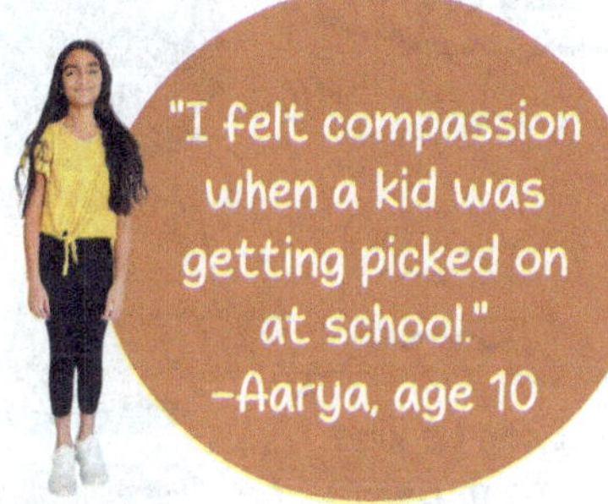

Write or draw about a time when you felt compassion for someone.

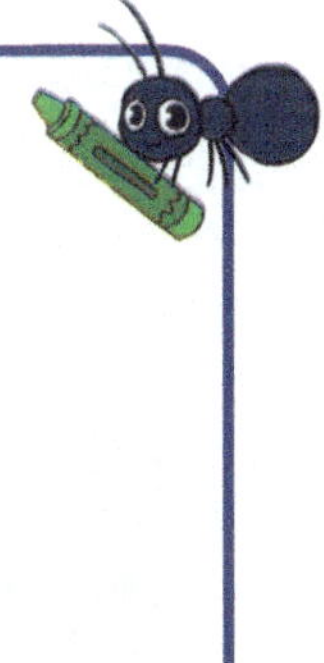

When you are struggling, you can be a friend to yourself by practicing the three parts of compassion:

1. Notice you are struggling
2. Remember connection (other kids sometimes struggle, too)
3. Self-kindness

Draw a line to match the picture with the resilience animal (you can use the definitions above to help). Then try the gestures for the three parts.

Spots, Buddy, and Snuggles have helpful habits. When you are struggling you can try one, two, or all three animal habits!

Not being able to fly is hard for you. Would you like to try the three parts of self-compassion?
Okay.
1. It's hard not being able to fly.
2. I'm not the only creature who can't fly.
Self-compassion and self-pity are not the same. Self-compassion helps us be mindful and remember we are not alone.
3. I'm still a good dragon.
Remember you are always good inside.

Activity 4.3 Tell the Bunny

For this activity, ask a grown-up to help you watch this play made by real kids:https://jamielynntatera.com/staying-close-story.

When Flame's blocks come tumbling down, the Feelings and Resilience Animals offer ideas to help. But Snuggles helps Flame without words. Even without a cape, the Snuggles habit can be a super power!

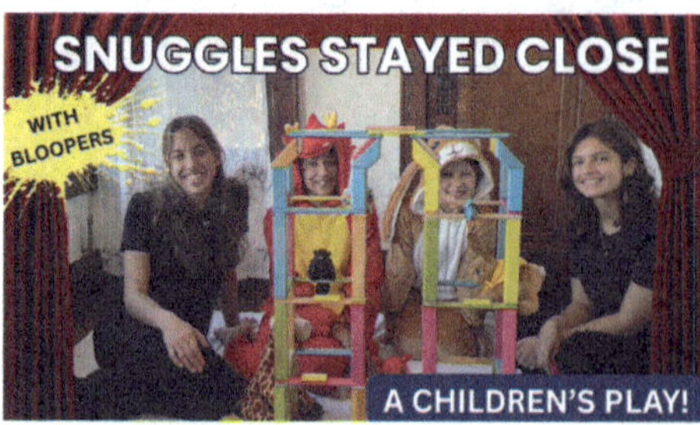

Self-compassion invites us to be like Snuggles–to allow ourselves to have all our feelings and be kind to ourselves.

Flame felt sad. What is something that you feel sad about? In the bunny below, you can share all your thoughts and all your feelings, and the bunny will just listen.

I care about you.

Activity 4.4 Three for Me

We are going to do a "three for me" practice using the three parts of self-compassion: noticing struggle (hands on head), connection (hands extended), and kindness (self-hug or other kind gesture).

To do this practice, we will need to think about a down moment. You can use the same idea that you told the bunny in the last activity, or another idea:

- ☐ You felt a little left out
- ☐ You didn't do well on a project
- ☐ You were stressed because you were late for something
- ☐ Other ______________________________

You can do Three for Me on your own, or you can ask an adult to read it to you or help you listen to an audio recording at: https://jamielynntatera.com/workbook-for-kids-guided-practices/

Three for Me:

To start, you can think about your difficult moment and notice how you feel. Now we can place our hands on our head and say to ourselves, 'This is hard.' This is the first part of 'Three for Me,' which is mindfulness. You can try different words to see what works for you.

- **Ouch!**
- **This is yucky!**
- **Ugh!**
- **Other ______________**

Circle the words that you would like.

Now we can extend our palms out and say, 'Having difficult moments is part of being human.' You can try other words to see what helps you feel connected to others.

- **It's okay to feel this way**
- **Other kids might feel like this too**
- **I am not alone**
- **Other ______________**

I'm your Buddy.

Now if you like, you can give yourself a hug or another kind gesture. You can also say kind words.

- It's going to be okay.
- I am here for you.
- You can do hard things.
- Other ______________

Think of words you might say to a friend if they were feeling sad, and then try saying those words to yourself.

If you haven't yet, you can circle your favorite words for each of the three parts of "Three for Me."

Note: We don't *have* to move our hands when we do this, but it can help us to remember the three parts.

This guided practice is used in the Self-Compassion for Children and Caregivers program and has been adapted from the adult Mindful Self-Compassion program.

How are you feeling now?

Nice

Okay

Uncomfortable

Mixed

Which part of Three for Me (hands on head, hands extended, or self-kindness) felt the best to you? Was there a part that was a little tricky?

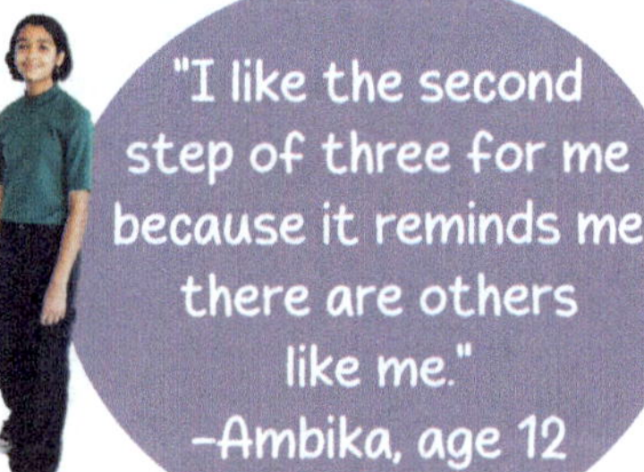

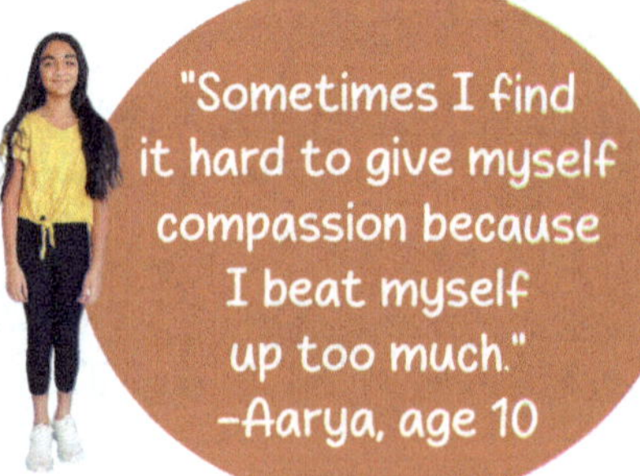

You may have noticed that it's kind of hard to be with tricky feelings. We are in Magic Mountains, and sometimes it feels hard to climb a mountain. But it feels really good when you get to the top of the mountain. You can do hard things. I believe in you!

Adventure 4 Take-Aways

Resilience Habit Animals

 = Buddy - I'm not alone / It's okay to feel this way

 = Spots - Noticing your five senses, feelings, or thoughts

 = Sunny - Thinking of good things

 = Snuggles - Comforting or encouraging words or touch

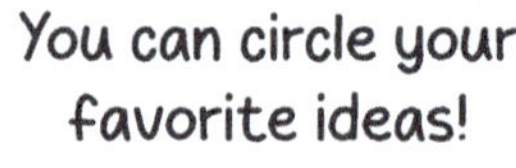

Ideas:

 Self-compassion is being kind to yourself when you are struggling.

  There are three parts of self-compassion: noticing our struggle, remembering we are not alone, and being kind to ourselves.

Helpful Practices:

  Tell the Bunny (journal or draw your feelings and thoughts when something tricky happens).

   Three for Me practice:

The three parts are hands on head (I'm struggling), hands outstretched (I'm connected), and self-hug (I'm kind to myself).

Bonus Activity:

Get some toys or stuffed animals and act out the story, The Rabbit Listened (from Activity 4.3).

Curiosity Question:

How would you like a friend to treat you when you feel sad?

A Note for Grown-Ups:
When a child is struggling, you can respond to them using the three parts of compassion. You can name their struggle, validate how they feel, and be kind to them. You can also do this for yourself!

CELEBRATE
You did it!
So great!!
Read the Scroll
Activity 4.1
Activity 4.2
Activity 4.3
Activity 4.4
Take-Aways
You are practicing
self-compassion! Here's a
cupcake for our party and a
rainbow for the magic potion
that will go in our cake.
HALFWAY THROUGH!!
S
S

In our next adventure, we'll visit the Land of Values.
Values
Self-Acceptance
Courage
Magic
Values give life meaning. What do you value?
I value kindness.
I value taking helpful actions!

I'm so mad that Billy is working with Sam instead of me.
I can tell you're really upset.
Yeah! I can't believe Billy did that!
I'm a little curious. What are you feeling under your anger? Are you feeling lonely or sad or disappointed?
I'm sad
You feel sad because something really matters. Are you wishing to have friendship or trust or belonging?
I guess I want to belong.
That makes sense. We all want to belong.
Often there's more than just anger. Exploring what's under anger can help us discover what really matters.

Everyone feels angry sometimes. What do you get mad about?
James felt mad that his friend was working with a different kid.
I feel mad that I can't fly like the other dragons.
I get mad when I lose something. -Marcos, age 11
I feel mad when people say things about me behind my back. -Sofia, age 14
You
You are entering the Land of Values

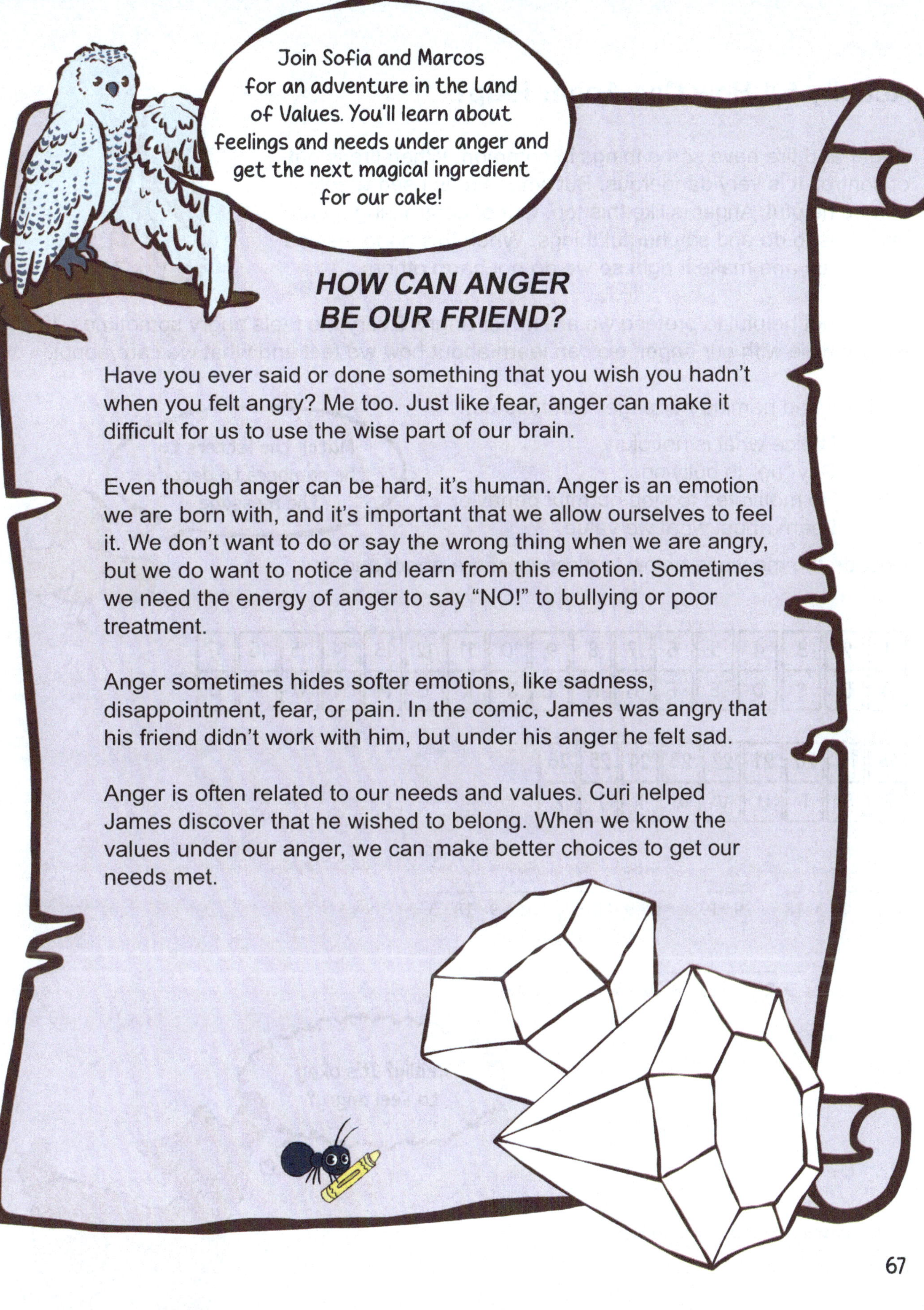

HOW CAN ANGER BE OUR FRIEND?

Have you ever said or done something that you wish you hadn't when you felt angry? Me too. Just like fear, anger can make it difficult for us to use the wise part of our brain.

Even though anger can be hard, it's human. Anger is an emotion we are born with, and it's important that we allow ourselves to feel it. We don't want to do or say the wrong thing when we are angry, but we do want to notice and learn from this emotion. Sometimes we need the energy of anger to say "NO!" to bullying or poor treatment.

Anger sometimes hides softer emotions, like sadness, disappointment, fear, or pain. In the comic, James was angry that his friend didn't work with him, but under his anger he felt sad.

Anger is often related to our needs and values. Curi helped James discover that he wished to belong. When we know the values under our anger, we can make better choices to get our needs met.

Activity 5.1 How Can Anger Help?

Anger and fire have some things in common. When fire is out of control, it is very dangerous. But when fire is used wisely, it can be helpful. Anger is like this too. Out of control anger can cause us to do and say hurtful things. When this happens, we want to try and make it right so we do not harm others.

But it's not helpful to pretend we are never angry. Everyone feels angry sometimes. If we are wise with our anger, we can learn about how we feel and what we care about.

Noticing and naming our anger can help us...

- Notice what is not okay
- Say "no" to bullying
- Be motivated to stop harmful behavior
- Learn about what we value

Match the letters to the numbers to decode the message.

Decode the message below to discover more about anger.

1	2	3	4	5	6	7	8	9	10	11	12	13	14	15	16	17
A	B	C	D	E	F	G	H	I	J	K	L	M	N	O	P	Q

18	19	20	21	22	23	24	25	26
R	S	T	U	V	W	X	Y	Z

_ _ _ _ _   _ _   _ _ _ _   _ _ _ _.
1 14 7 5 18   9 19   12 9 11 5   6 9 18 5

_ _ _   _ _   _ _ _ _   _ _ _ _.
21 19 5   9 20   23 9 20 8   3 1 18 5

Anger is like fire. Use it with care.

Activity 5.2 Shake it Off

Before we can use anger wisely, we need to observe it. Anger includes both thoughts in our mind and sensations in our body.

It can be helpful to pay attention to the sensations of anger in your body. Which parts of your body get tight when you feel angry? What happens to your breathing?

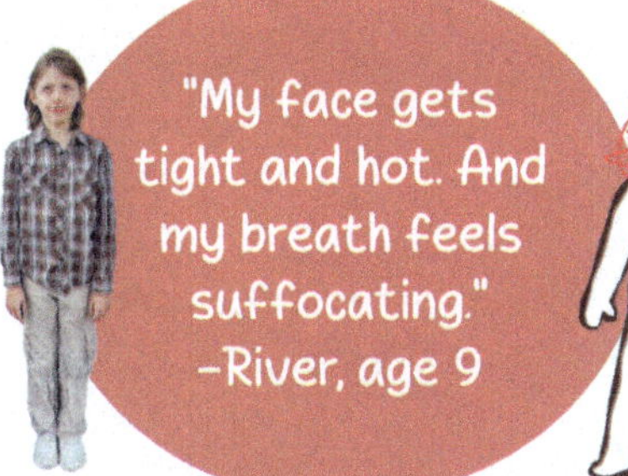

Think of a situation when you felt mad at someone. Remember some details so that you can feel anger in your body.

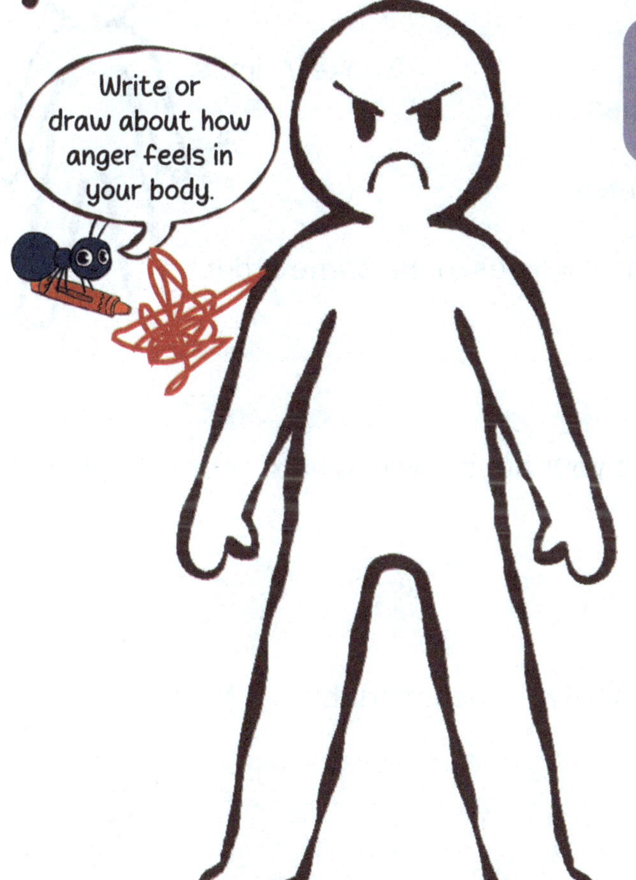

Let yourself be with anger's sensations. Can you also feel your feet?

After feeling and accepting anger, we can find a safe way to release angry energy. It is usually helpful to release angry energy before deciding what to do about it.

Here are a couple ideas that you can try to release angry energy:

Angry Scribbles: Grab a crayon and scribble your anger in this box.

Shake Off Your Anger

Note: You can make noises while you shake if you want to.

Shake 7 times

Start by standing and feeling your feet.
Now shake one of your legs seven times.
Then your other leg seven times.
Now shake one of your arms seven times.
And then your other arm.
Now shake each of your legs and arms six times in the same order.
Then five times,
Now four times…
Three, two, one.
Then shake your whole body.
Finally, stretch up and yawn, then drop your arms down toward your feet. Repeat stretching up and down two more times.

How was shaking it off?

Nice

Okay

Uncomfortable

Mixed

Some kids release angry energy through breathing. You could try five finger breathing or deep breaths like cookie breathing (see our first Land for these practices).

Some kids like to move when they feel angry. Other kids like to yell into a pillow. Some kids like to take deep breaths. How do you like to safely release your angry energy?

____

____

When I think about not being able to fly, I get so mad that I start to breathe fire!

That's intense! Do you want to shake off your anger?

Being tired or hungry can make anger stronger. If you are tired or hungry while being angry, it helps to have a snack or get some rest.

In the Land of Sensations (in book 1), we learned to squeeze and soften body parts to release stress. We tightened a body part, held our breath, and then softened the body part while we breathed out our mouth. You can also try this exercise with angry feelings.

Activity 5.3 What's Under Anger

Now that we've felt angry sensations and safely released angry energy, we're ready to learn from our anger. Anger is a hard emotion that can hide softer emotions and needs.

Here's Khalil's story of layers of feelings and needs under anger:

"I was playing kickball, and my friends wouldn't let me keep playing. I felt angry. Under my anger, I felt left out and lonely. I was wishing for friendship and belonging."

Our bodies get tight when we feel angry because anger is a hard, protective emotion. Khalil was feeling angry. **We can imagine that anger is a box.**

Under anger, there are often soft emotions, like sadness, disappointment, fear, loneliness, or hurt. **Under his anger, Khalil felt lonely and left out.**

Under soft feelings, we can find values and needs that all humans share, like choice, freedom, and friendship. Khalil was wishing for friendship and belonging. **We can imagine that our values and needs are like jewels.**

What softer feelings and needs do you have under your anger about not being able to fly?

I'm not sure.

I know how that is.

Let's help Flame think about hidden feelings and values.

Flame feels angry about not being able to fly. What soft feelings do you think Flame could have under the anger? If you're not sure about the layers, just be curious!!

These are common "soft" feelings that hide under anger.
Circle all the feelings Flame might have.

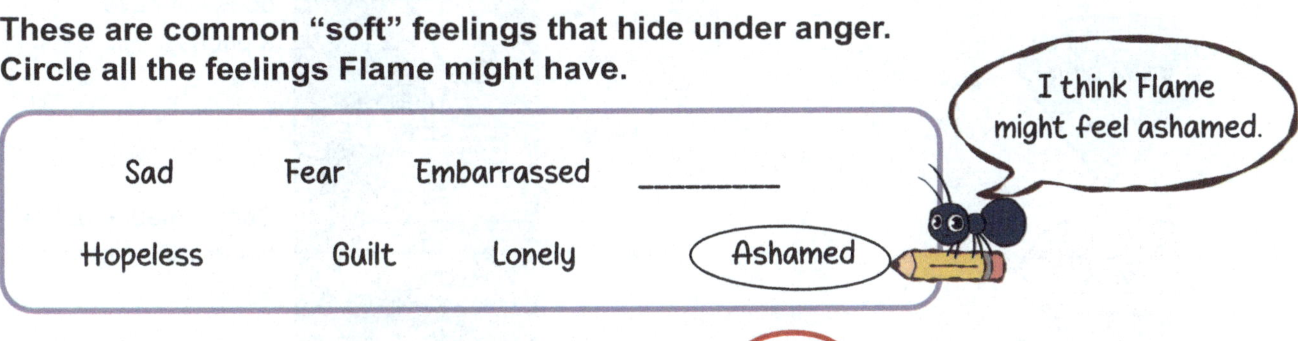

These are some needs that can hide under anger. Circle what could Flame be wishing for.

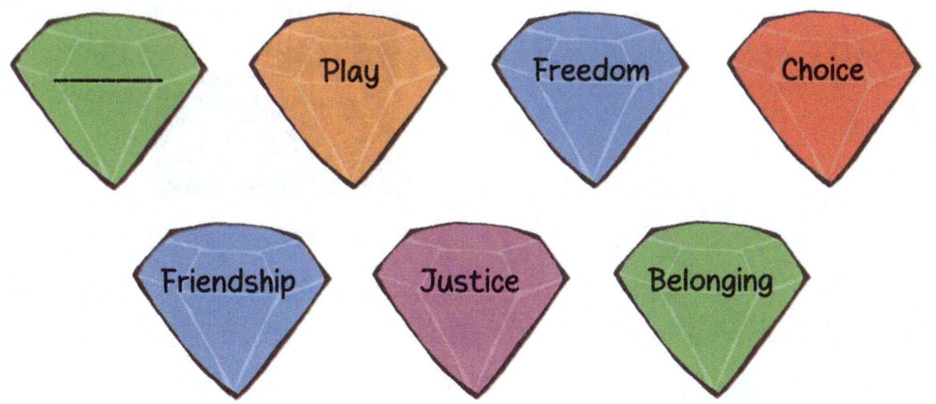

Activity 5.4 Guess My Need

Our values and needs are like the "flame" of anger that we want to pay attention to. Once we know what we need, we can get curious about how our needs can be met.

In the comics that follow, the characters are mad. Underneath their anger, there are values and needs.

What could the characters be wishing for?

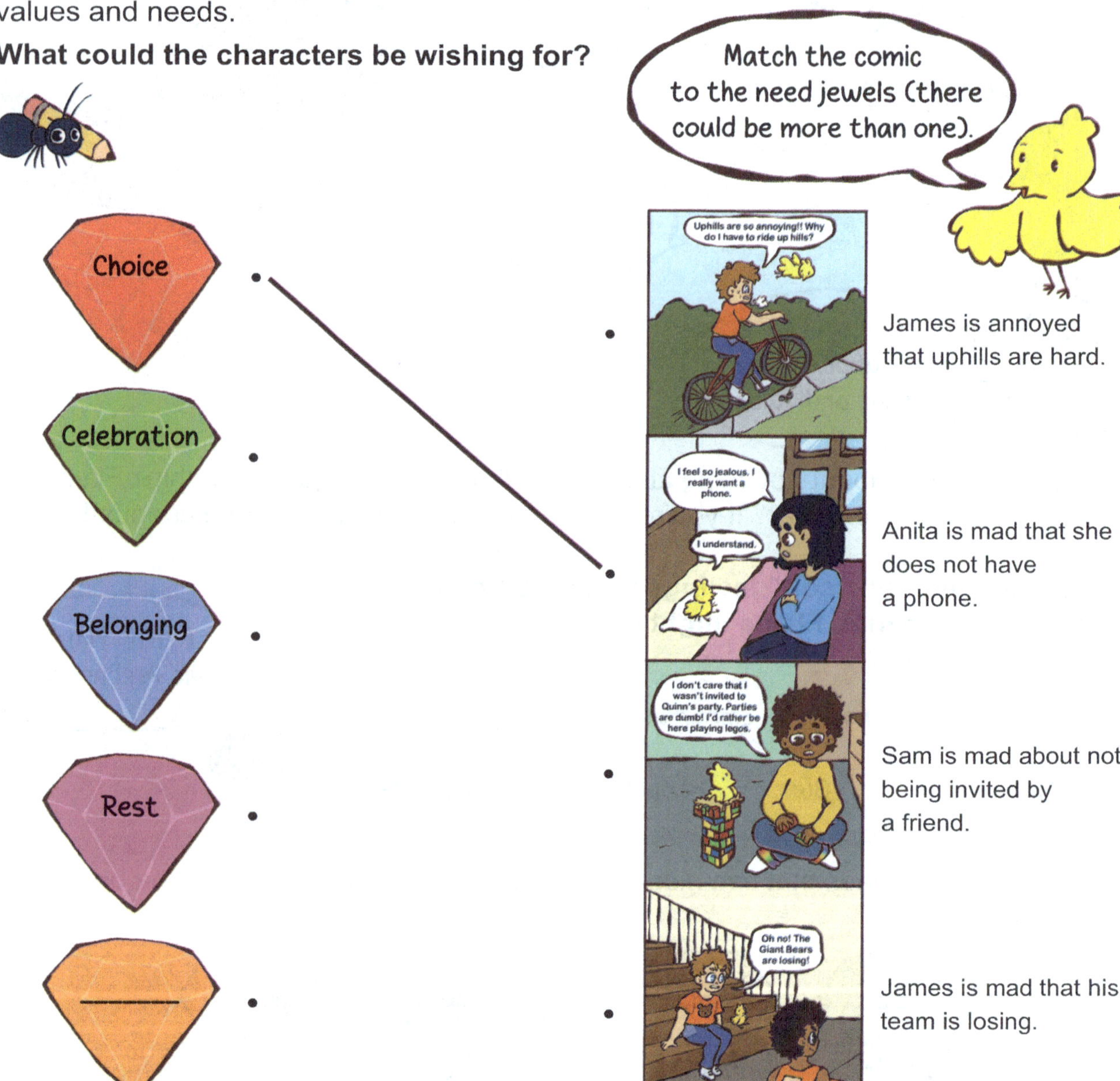

Don't worry if you aren't sure about the answers. There could be different needs for different people, and we would have to ask the characters to really be sure.

Adventure 5 Take-Aways

Resilience Habit Animals

 = Buddy - I'm not alone / It's okay to feel this way

 = Spots - Noticing your five senses, feelings, or thoughts

 = Sunny - Thinking of good things

 = Snuggles - Comforting or encouraging words or touch

 = Doodles - Actions that are kind to your body, mind or heart

Ideas:

 Everyone gets mad sometimes.

 Anger can be a protective force when used wisely.

 Exploring layers under anger, such as soft feelings and needs, can help us create happier relationships.

Helpful Practices:

 Notice sensations of anger in the body while also noticing the bottoms of your feet.

 Get curious about the soft feelings and wishes hiding under anger.

Bonus Activity:

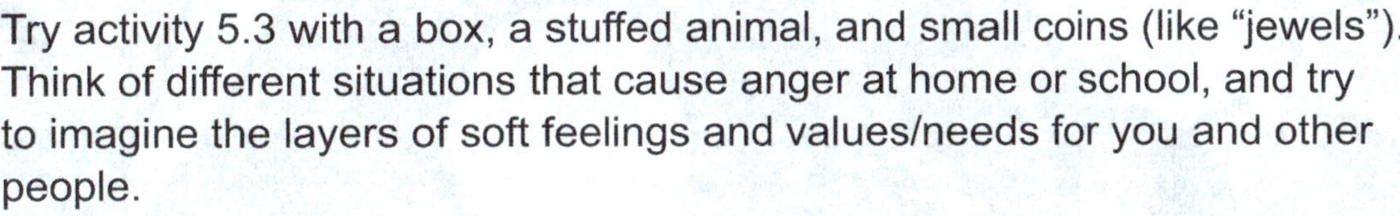

Try activity 5.3 with a box, a stuffed animal, and small coins (like "jewels"). Think of different situations that cause anger at home or school, and try to imagine the layers of soft feelings and values/needs for you and other people.

Curiosity Question:

What soft feelings or needs are most often under your anger?

A Note for Grown-Ups:
When adults and kids feel angry, sometimes they need to vent before they are ready to focus on soft feelings and needs. Investigating children's needs under anger and getting curious about strategies to meet needs can increase kids' sense of agency and connectedness to others.

CELEBRATE
It's amazing how much you're learning!
Read the Scroll
Activity 5.1
Activity 5.2
Activity 5.3
Activity 5.4
Take-Aways
You are discovering values under anger. Here's a cupcake for our party and gems for our magic potion!
YOU'RE DOING GREAT!

In our last adventure in Foundation Forest, we'll visit the Land of Self-Acceptance.

I don't know why my mom keeps making me play soccer. I'm not good at it, and I don't like it!
That sounds hard. We can practice to get better, but there will still be things we struggle with.
I'm not very good at soccer either.
That's because you're a bird!
I know! Each of us is created to do and be something special. We will do some things well and struggle with other things. I can build nests very well.
What is something you're good at?
I'm good at my Lego creations. I make lego builds that come straight from my imagination.
That's so awesome! Your lego creations are special, and so are you. We are each a unique and unrepeatable creation!

We are each a unique creation. What is something special about you?

PERFECTLY IMPERFECT

In the comic, Sam was upset about being forced to play soccer even though Sam was not interested or skilled at it. Curi helped Sam realize that we all have a unique mix of strengths and weaknesses.

Sometimes kids tell themselves that they should be perfect. No one is perfect! Nobody is good at everything! Even though we can improve at things, we will still fall short sometimes.

When we fail at something, we might feel frustrated with ourselves. We might think something is wrong with us and feel ashamed. We feel shame because we want to be loved and approved of by others, but shame is hard. We can remind ourselves that everyone falls short sometimes, and we are not alone with our struggles.

We can accept (and even love!) the unique mixture of strengths and struggles that each of us has.

Activity 6.1 Strengths and Struggles

Sometimes it's hard to remember that everyone has ways they are strong and ways they struggle.

Think of a friend or someone you like to spend time with.

I like to spend time with Buddy!

Write their name or draw a picture of this person in the box below:

Now think of a word that you can use to describe your friend. **Write down a word or sentence that describes them.**

Did you write down something good about your friend?

- ☐ Yes
- ☐ No

My friend is good at everything!!

Many people think about their friends' good qualities. We can appreciate what is good about our friends.

Your friend also has some ways that they struggle–everyone struggles! Maybe your friend is not good at a sport or a subject at school. Maybe they sometimes have a hard time sharing or interrupt you. **Write down one way your friend struggles.**

Could you think of a way that your friend struggles? It might seem strange to think about their weaknesses, but everyone has both good qualities and ways they fall short.

It's hard for me to think of things I'm good at.

Just like your friend, you have both strengths and struggles, too. Think of one of your good qualities or something you are good at (at least some of the time). **Write down one of your strengths below.**

_ _

_ _

Remember, everyone has good qualities, including you!

We might wish that we had only good qualities and no weaknesses, but that's not how humans are made. Everyone falls short sometimes, including you. Maybe you struggle with a sport or a subject at school, or maybe sometimes you have a hard time sharing. **Write down one way that you sometimes struggle.**

_ _

_ _

"In my homework, I struggle with missing assignments." -Marcos, age 11

"It felt odd to talk about my weaknesses, but I felt better after talking about it." -Khalil, age 8

We can meet our struggles with self-compassion and remember that everyone has challenges. It's good to be on the learning team along with everyone else!

**This exercise has been adapted from the Mindfulness and Self-Compassion for Children and Caregivers program.*

Activity 6.2 Less than, Greater than, Equal to

Comparing ourselves to others can be like math.

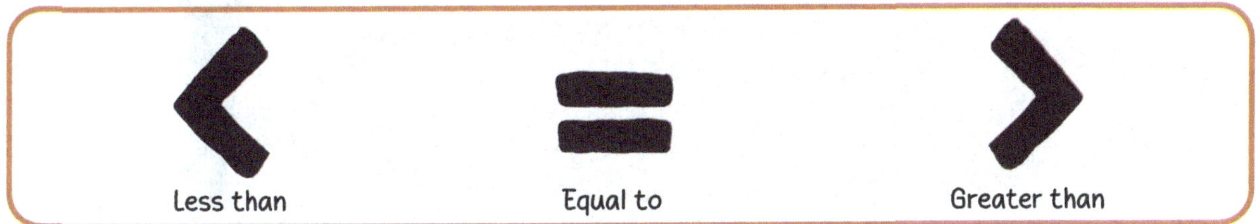

The connecting part of self-compassion is like the equal sign. When we remember that everyone has strengths and struggles, we feel connected.

Less than and greater than thoughts both make us feel separate from others.

We can transform our "greater than" thoughts (I'm a better person) and "less than" thoughts (I'm not a good enough person) into equal to thoughts: we all have good things that we can celebrate and areas where we fall short.

Here's an example of Matteo having greater than thought:

> "In baseball I thought I was better than everyone. But then I joined a different group, and some of them were better than me."
> -Matteo, age 8

On his first baseball team, Matteo had more skills, but he wasn't a better person. Matteo's greater than thought created a feeling of being different.

Matteo's equal to thought created connection.

Can you think of a time when you had a greater than thought?

____

____

Here's an example of Maya having a less than thought:

> "When I was in fourth grade everyone finished reading their article, and they could understand and answer the questions. I couldn't even read the article and I didn't know how to answer the questions. I felt alone and not good enough." –Maya, age 14

Maya has dyslexia and struggles with reading, but she isn't a worse person. Maya's less than thought made her feel alone.

Maya's equal to thought made her feel more connected.

An equal thought does not mean that we pretend that we all have the same skills (an untrue thought). Instead it helps us remember that we are all on the learning team with more skills in some areas and less skills in others, and we are all equally valuable.

Can you think of a time when you had a less than thought?

____

____

Activity 6.3 Transforming Our Thoughts

We can notice our greater than, less than and equal to thoughts. It is natural to have these thoughts. When we have a greater than or less than thought, we can create a more connecting thought and remind ourselves we are all human beings with strengths and struggles.

Match the comic to the greater than, less than, or equal to sign.

Equal To

Connection

Less Than

No Connection

Greater Than

No Connection

Remember a time when you had a less than or a greater than thought (I'm not good enough, or I'm better than them). Write your less than or greater than thought in the thought bubble. Then, create an "equal to" thought that can help you feel more connected to others.

Activity 6.4 Our Pieces

Each of us is like a puzzle with different pieces. We are strong at some things and struggle with others. We have parts of us that feel proud of our accomplishments, and parts of us that are frustrated or embarrassed about the ways we fall short. We are growing a compassionate self that can hold all of our pieces with love.

River (from the Kids' Team) filled in his puzzle pieces with different things about himself, things that he is good at and struggles he has.

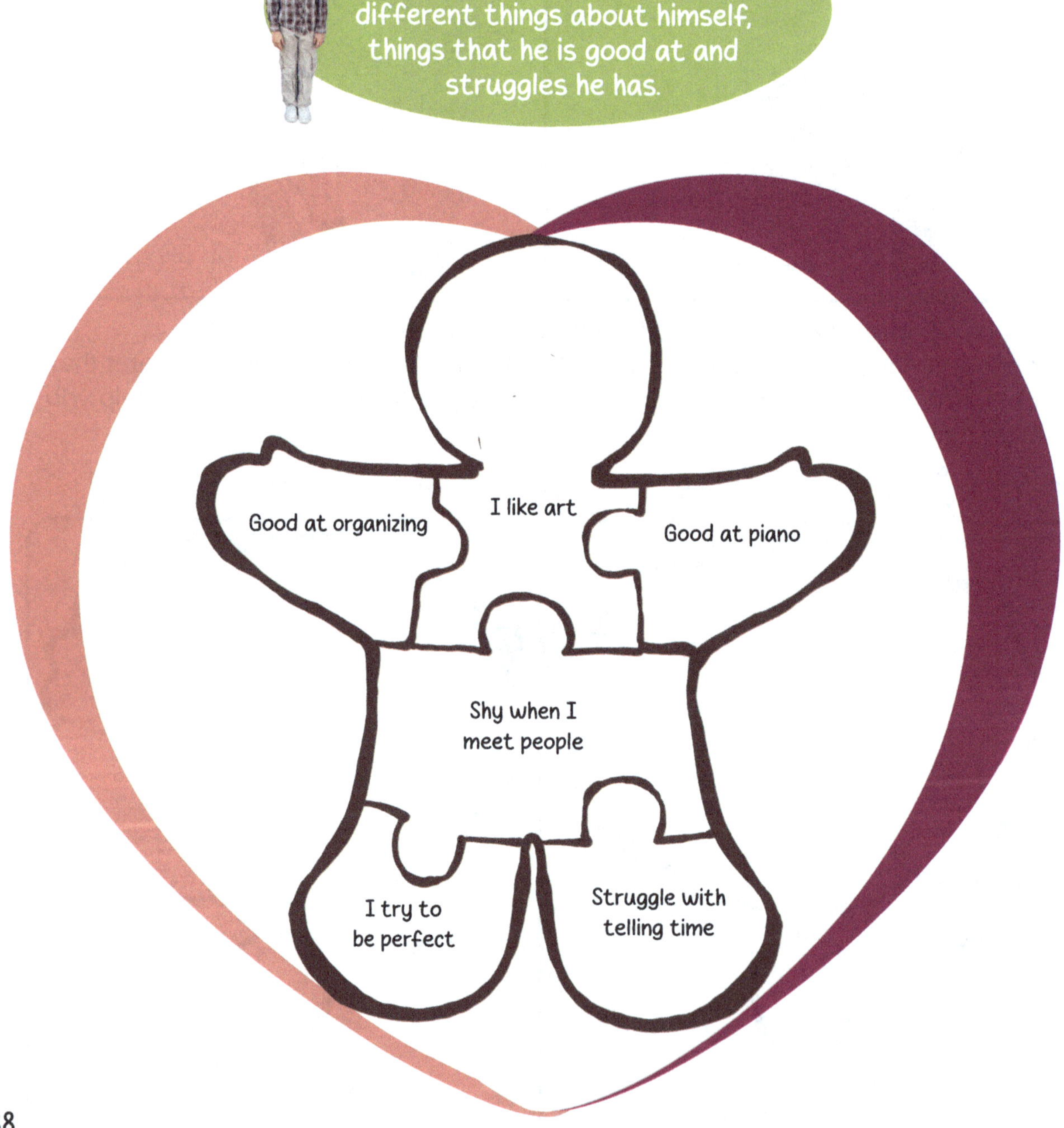

Fill out your pieces. Be sure to include things you're good at and things you struggle with because they are all part of you!

Write both your strengths and struggles in your pieces.

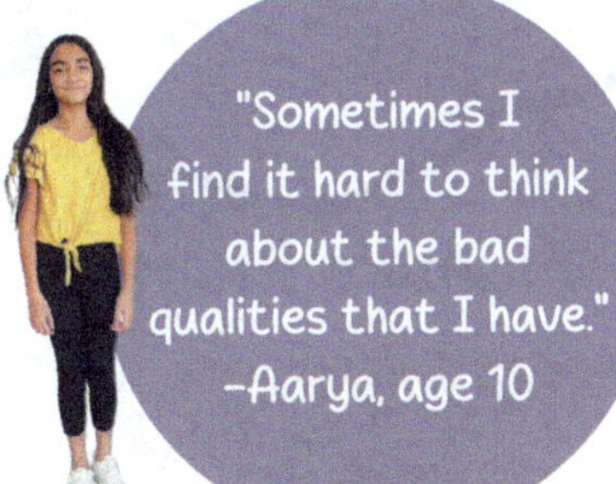

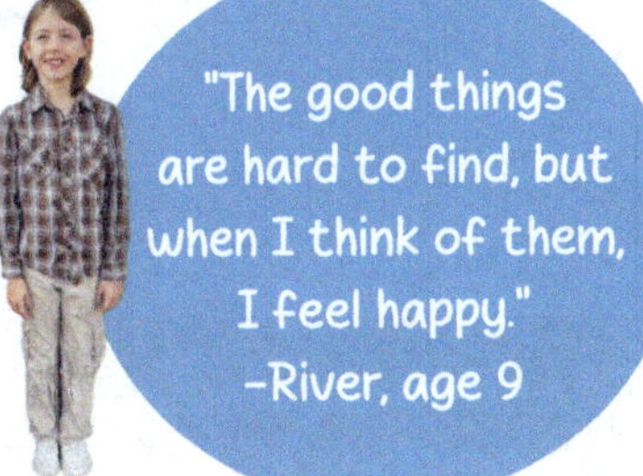

Flame's Pieces

It's self-compassionate to appreciate our strengths, and hold our struggles with compassion.

Adventure 6 Take-Aways

You can circle your favorite ideas!

Resilience Habit Animals

 = Buddy - I'm not alone / It's okay to feel this way

 = Spots - Noticing your five senses, feelings, or thoughts

 = Sunny - Thinking of good things

 = Snuggles - Comforting or encouraging words or touch

Ideas:

 We all have good qualities and struggles. Self-compassion invites us to love and accept our whole selves.

 We can transform "less than" and "greater than" thoughts into "equal" thoughts by remembering that others, too, have strengths and weaknesses.

Helpful Practices:

 When you fall short, remind yourself that everyone has strengths and struggles, including you.

 Notice and love all of your pieces.

Bonus Activity:

In addition to giving ourselves compassion for our weaknesses, we can also appreciate our strengths. Draw a picture or write a note about something that you like about yourself. Sometimes this is hard for people, and you can ask a grown-up for ideas. You are an amazing person, and it's kind to appreciate yourself.

Curiosity Question:

Can something be both a strength and a weakness at the same time?

A Note for Grown-Ups:
Sharing your strengths and struggles with children is a powerful way to teach them to do the same. When you are being hard on yourself because you have fallen short, you can normalize the inner critic by sharing your struggles, and then model a more compassionate response. It's helpful to start with self-acceptance, and if you need support to grow and change, you can model that too.

CELEBRATE
You are a self-acceptance super star!
Read the Scroll
Activity 6.1
Activity 6.2
Activity 6.3
Activity 6.4
Take-Aways
You are learning to accept yourself as you are. Here's a cupcake for our party and heart energy for our magic potion!
ALMOST THROUGH THE MOUNTAINS!
S

In the next adventure, we'll visit the Land of Courage.

TALENT SHOW sign up
I really want to play piano in the talent show, but I don't think I'm good enough.
If one of your friends was scared to play in the talent show, what would you say to your friend?
I would tell them that they can do it and that I believe in them!
Those are encouraging words! Can you say that to yourself?
Sure!
I can do it. I'll try my best.
Woo!!
Wow!
Clap's
Even though a part of you is afraid you are not good enough, there is another part that can help you to try and do your best.

It can feel scary to try something new or hard. Are there things you dream of doing that seem challenging?
Anita dreamed of playing in the talent show.
I dream of running the Tunnel Race!
I dream of being able to do a triple axel while ice skating. –Khalil, age 8
I dream of being an actor. –Anjali, age 10
AXOLOTL
Just a GRL who loves ACTING
You
You are entering the Land of Courage

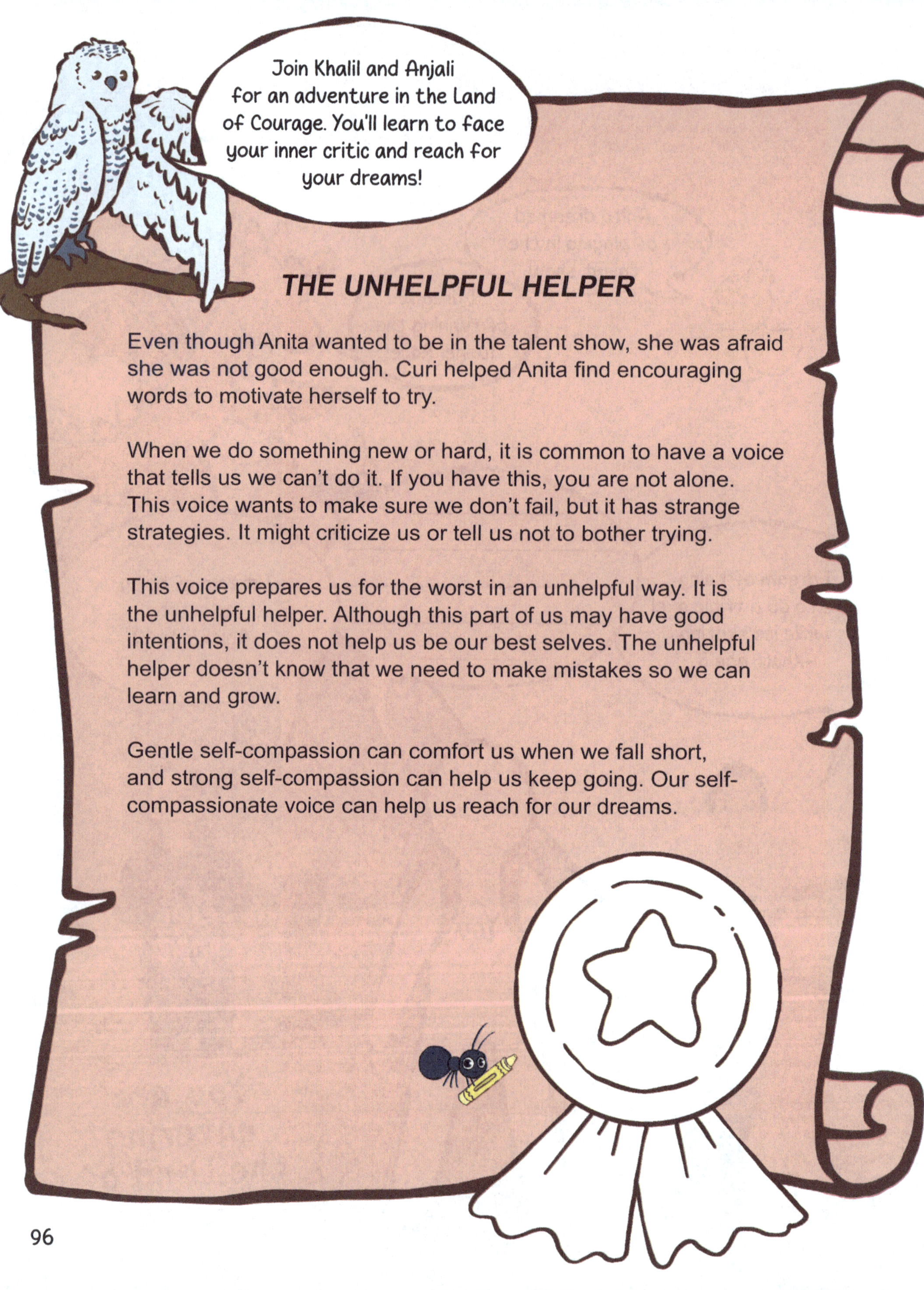

THE UNHELPFUL HELPER

Even though Anita wanted to be in the talent show, she was afraid she was not good enough. Curi helped Anita find encouraging words to motivate herself to try.

When we do something new or hard, it is common to have a voice that tells us we can't do it. If you have this, you are not alone. This voice wants to make sure we don't fail, but it has strange strategies. It might criticize us or tell us not to bother trying.

This voice prepares us for the worst in an unhelpful way. It is the unhelpful helper. Although this part of us may have good intentions, it does not help us be our best selves. The unhelpful helper doesn't know that we need to make mistakes so we can learn and grow.

Gentle self-compassion can comfort us when we fall short, and strong self-compassion can help us keep going. Our self-compassionate voice can help us reach for our dreams.

Activity 7.1 The Unhelpful Helper

Many of us have an inner voice that tries to "help" us avoid failure with unhelpful strategies, like self-doubt and self-criticism ("Why even try?" or "You're no good!").

Abbie (from the Kids' Team) has an unhelpful helper that talks to her when she draws. Her unhelpful helper says things like, "You should stop now." "You should quit." "You're really bad at this." "Erase it all!" **If Abbie believes her unhelpful helper, she stops drawing.**

When Abbie realizes her unhelpful helper is shutting her down, she doesn't listen to its words and ideas. She is growing a compassionate voice that helps her to keep drawing.

"In music class the unhelpful helper says that it hates me because no one thinks I'm a good singer."
–Dallas, age 7

"The Unhelpful Helper loves you and tries to protect you, but not in wise ways."
–River, age 9

It can be fun to create a character and nickname for your unhelpful helper. Abbie drew a character and nicknamed her unhelpful helper Angie (see her drawing below).

Angie (Abbie's Unhelpful Helper)

If you're like me, you're afraid that your drawing won't be good enough!

Make a silly drawing of your "unhelpful helper," and write their nickname.

What is your unhelpful helper's nickname? ____________________

"Sometimes I believe my unhelpful helper. But then I tell someone, and they encourage me."
–Maya, age 14

"Instead of an unhelpful helper and a helpful helper, it seems like a devil and an angel whispering into my ears."
–Abbie, age 12

"In art class I used to get mad at myself because my art wasn't perfect. I would get so angry that I would rip my paper. Then I would feel ashamed of myself for ripping it and wish I could hide. Now I ask for a new paper, or I keep drawing and whisper a song to myself, 'Every little thing is gonna be alright.'"
–River, age 9

When your unhelpful helper starts imagining the worst or criticizing you, you can picture your character and call them by their nickname. Even though it's trying to help you, you don't have to follow its advice!

Activity 7.2 Caring Owl

Self-compassion involves balancing self-acceptance with a desire to grow and change in healthy ways. The unhelpful helper uses harsh judgments and words, but we can develop a kind and wise self, like a caring owl. **Our caring owl sees our strengths and weaknesses clearly, loves us, and can help us be our best selves.**

You can color your caring owl that loves you and all your pieces.

Choose silly or interesting words from the below categories and write them in the lines.

Difficult Emotion 1 (feeling) _______________

Adjective (describes something) _____________

Adverb (describes an action) ________________

Color _______________

Noun (thing) _________________

Difficult Emotion 2 (feeling) ______________

Name of Your Unhelpful Helper ______________

Pronoun (he, she, it, they) ______________

Plural Noun (things) ____________________

Room in Your House ________________

Now write the words that you chose in the story:

Today I was feeling _________________ (difficult emotion 1). It was because today was a very _______________ (adjective) day, and people were acting _____________ (adverb).

Then the _______________ (color) owl came and knocked on my ____________ (noun).

I let the owl in, and it said, "I love you, and I see you are ________________ (difficult emotion 2)."

Then _______________ (Unhelpful Helper's name) came and said, "No, you are really bad, and you are going to fail at everything. I am just looking out for you." I felt ____________ (difficult emotion 1).

Then the owl said, "I'm sorry that ____________________ (pronoun) said that. You are loved no matter what." Later I was supposed to be doing my homework but I was watching ____________________ (plural noun) on TV. The wise and caring owl came into the ______________________ (room in your house), and said, "I think that you should do your homework because then you won't have to do it later during recess. I love you."

That day I realized that the ___________ (color) owl really loved me.

If you'd like, you can make a drawing or comic about your story.

Sometimes we have unhelpful behaviors that prevent us from being our best selves. We might play too many video games, not get enough sleep, avoid our homework, or eat unhealthy foods. Our wise and compassionate owl can lovingly support the ways that we need to grow and change to become our best selves.

What is an unhelpful behavior that your wise and compassionate owl could help you try to change?

Pick a habit you'd really like to change.

____

____

"I procrastinate my homework by playing on my phone." -Maya, age 14

"I don't clean, and things get messy." -Dallas, age 7

"I should use less technology and Youtube." -Khalil, age 8

Activity 7.3 Crystal Ball

What are some things that you wish to do better or ways that you hope to grow and change? What would help you be the best version of yourself?

Imagine yourself growing in this way. In the crystal ball, draw (or write) yourself doing the activity the way you wish to do it.

You can replay your vision again and again. Imagining what you dream of is part of making your dream become real.

I want to run the Tunnel Race, but I'm afraid of the dark.
I will shine while you run.
You can notice your fear, and remember it's a false alarm.
You can DO it!
It can be hard to face your fears. I believe in you.
We will be there with you!

Activity 7.4 Inner Teammate

In the comic, Anita used the same words with herself that she would use to encourage a friend. Being self-compassionate means that we use kindness to help ourselves do our best.

Friends and teammates often use encouraging words to motivate each other. We can develop an inner teammate to motivate ourselves to move toward our goals and be the best version of ourselves.

Our inner teammate can help us reach our dreams by making a plan and using an encouraging voice.

Here's an example of a goal from the Kids' Team.

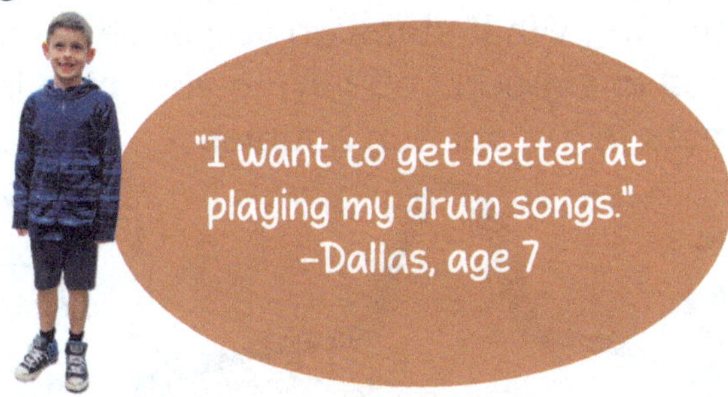

These are the steps and encouraging words that Dallas used to move toward his goal.

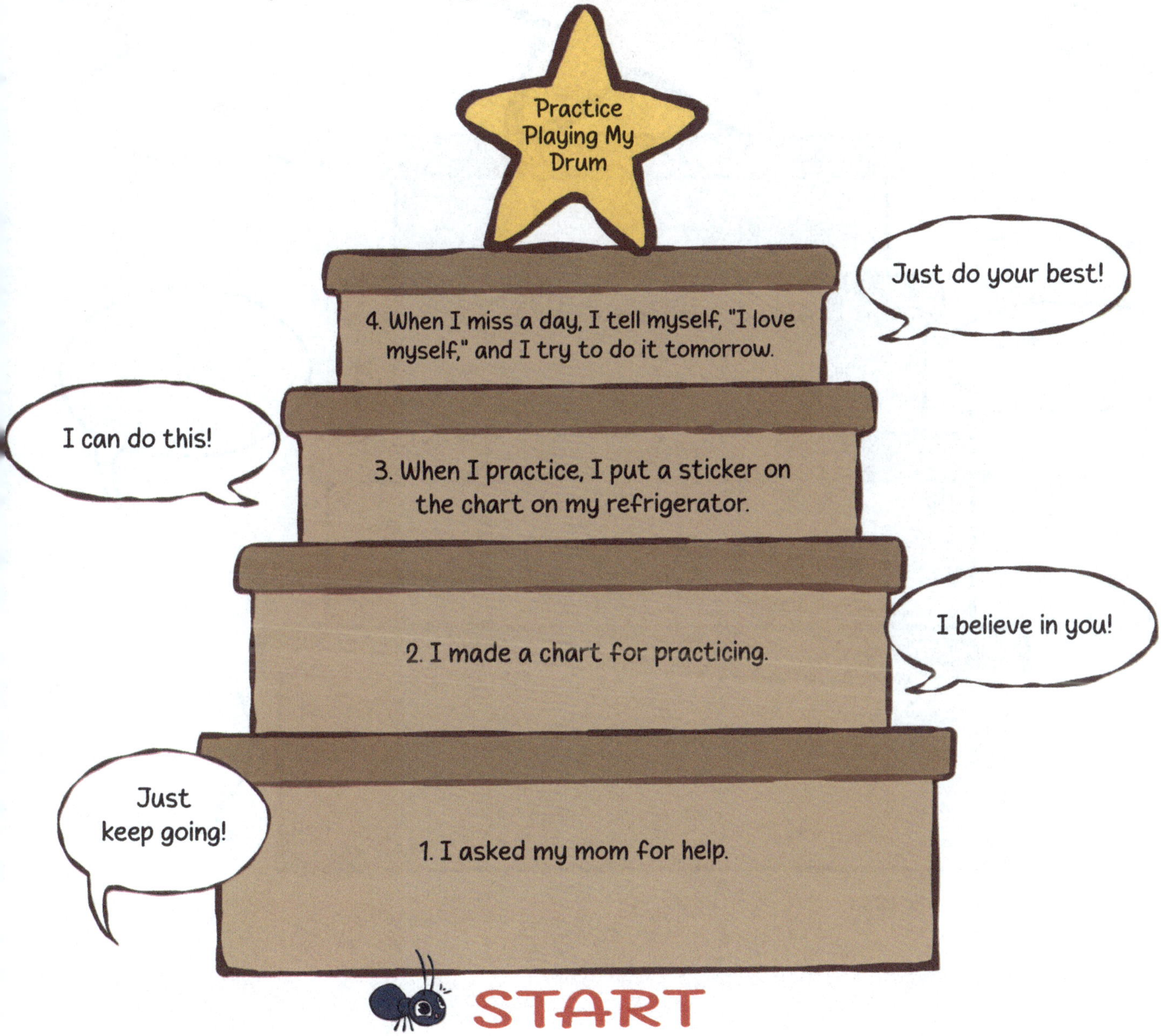

Practice Playing My Drum

Just do your best!

4. When I miss a day, I tell myself, "I love myself," and I try to do it tomorrow.

I can do this!

3. When I practice, I put a sticker on the chart on my refrigerator.

I believe in you!

2. I made a chart for practicing.

Just keep going!

1. I asked my mom for help.

START

What is your goal **(you can use the same goal from your crystal ball or pick a new one)**? Write your goal in the star. What steps do you need to take to reach your goal? What resources do you need to support you? Write your plan in the steps and the words of your inner teammate in the speech bubbles.

Sometimes you won't meet your goal, and you will need comforting self-compassion. Then your inner teammate can help you get back up and try again!

Flame's Plan
Run the Tunnel Race
Even though I feel afraid, I'll be okay.
I believe in myself!
4. I signed up for the Tunnel Race and invited my friends to watch me run.
Keep on going!
3. I ran through the tunnel by myself to practice, even though I felt afraid.
Just do your best!
2. I asked Buddy to go through the tunnel with me.
1. I started to run everyday.
I did it! I faced my fears and reached for my dreams!!
HOORAY!!
Barry
Flame

Adventure 7 Take-Aways

Resilience Habit Animals

 = Spots - Noticing your five senses, feelings, or thoughts

 = Sunny - Thinking of good things

 = Snuggles - Comforting or encouraging words or touch

 = Doodles - Actions that are kind to your body, mind or heart

Ideas and Practices:

 Your unhelpful helper wants to help you but uses poor strategies, like criticizing you or telling you not to bother trying.

 Your caring owl loves you as you are and wants to help you become your best self.

 Your inner teammate can help you make goals and encourage you to grow.

You can circle your favorite ideas!

Helpful Practices:

 Notice your unhelpful helper, and call them by their nickname.

 Imagine what your caring owl would say to you, and say those words to yourself.

 Pay attention to what you value and dream of.

 Make a plan and encourage yourself to grow and change in healthy ways. You can ask a trusted grown-up to help you.

Bonus Activity:

Strong / Supportive Gestures: Just like comforting gestures can soothe us when things go wrong, supportive gestures can help us feel strong (like Super Snuggles). Try different body movements to find what helps you feel strong. Some ideas include:

- Put your hands on your waist
- Make strong arms
- A fist on your heart
- Stand strong like a mountain
- Pat your back
- Other (your own idea!)

You can do a strong gesture when you want to help yourself do something brave.

Curiosity Question:

Who is someone that could help you reach your goals?

"Sometimes my biggest opportunity for growth is to love and accept myself as I am." -Jamie Lynn

CELEBRATE
You are growing so much!
Read the Scroll
Activity 7.1
Activity 7.2
Activity 7.3
Activity 7.4
Take-Aways
You are learning to help yourself reach goals with kindness! Here's a cupcake for our party and a gold medal for our magic potion!
WE FINISHED MAGIC MOUNTAINS!!

We need to add
our gold medal, value gems,
heart energy and rainbow to
make our magical self-
compassion potion.
I'll take the
potion to the island!

In our last adventure, we'll visit the Land of Celebration!

We need to carry the basket across the starfish bridge.
I will carry it!!!
No, Bear, you'll drop it. Let me carry it.
BUTTER
Not again...
OH NOO!!!!!
Chocolate Chips
BUTTER
FLOUR
Powdered Sugar
Honey
Milk
Baking So
Freeze-Dried Fruit

How do you feel about what just happened?
I can't believe we lost all our cake ingredients!
This is really hard. Would you like a hug?
I understand why you are upset. I bet the kids are upset, too.
What!!?? We wasted our time! -Dallas, age 7
I'm mad! We spent all these adventures working up to this, and now it's all ruined! -Maya, age 14
You
It makes sense if you feel upset. You worked really hard.

Self-compassion won't make difficult things go away, but it can help us to cope when hard things happen.

It's over now! They already lost!
Even though no team can win all the time, it's still disappointing.
Yeah. What can I do to feel better?
Talking about it can help. How else have you comforted yourself in the past?
Everyone sometimes feels difficult feelings.
I don't even know what I need right now.
Getting curious about what you need is its own kindness. Do you want to walk to the park?
Sure!

Sometimes kids aren't sure how to comfort themselves. What resilience habits are you trying to grow?
James was upset and wasn't sure how to comfort himself.
That happens to me ALL the time!
I'm trying to be kind to myself. –Matteo, age 8
I am trying to go grow Sunny and Spots so that I can see good things and also notice other things. –Aarya, age 10
You
You are entering the Land of Celebration

You might be having side-by-side feelings. We lost ingredients, which is sad. But we made it to our last adventure, which is happy.

What Works for You?

Congratulations! You've made it to our last adventure! You have learned so much - let yourself take in the goodness of how much you have grown.

Now, imagine you've just finished doing a basketball camp or taking a class in math, art, or some other subject. If you wanted to keep improving the skills you learned, would you need to practice? Of course you would!

The same is true with your resilience skills. You've learned a lot, and you will need to practice your self-compassion and resilience habits to strengthen them. In the comic, James was strengthening his skills when he wondered what he needed to do to help himself.

You can find ways to practice self-compassion that feel natural, but it might feel a little awkward at first. You can find a balance between doing what feels comfortable for you and continuing to grow.

You are an amazing person, and self-compassion can support you so you can enjoy your life!

Activity 8.1 Your Resilience Habit Animals

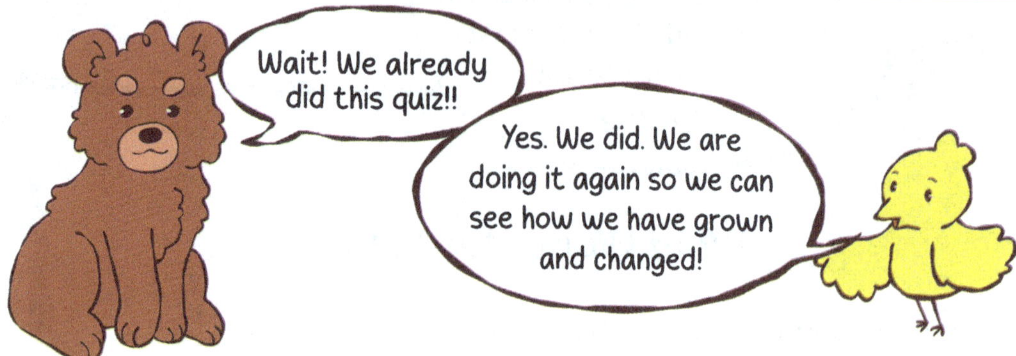

Which animal habits would you find helpful in the below situations? Any answer is great, and you can pick more than one.

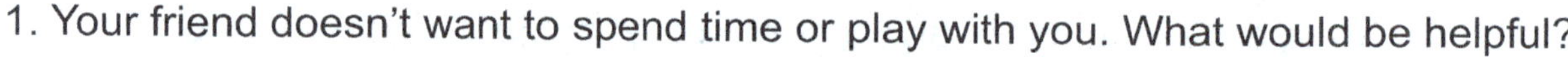
1. Your friend doesn't want to spend time or play with you. What would be helpful?
   -  Notice what you are thinking and feeling
   -  Remind yourself that these kinds of things happen sometimes
   - 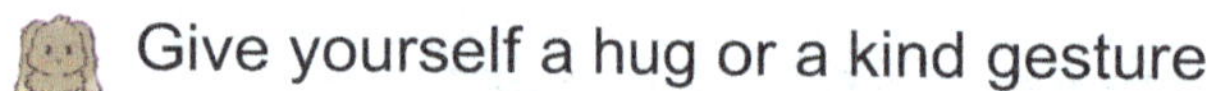 Give yourself a hug or a kind gesture
   - Do something you like to do
   - Listen to your favorite music or think of something good

2. You did poorly on something you worked hard on. What would be helpful?.
   - Notice your emotions and how your body feels
   - Remember that everyone struggles sometimes
   - Tell yourself it's a bummer, and you'll try again next time
   - Tell someone and/or learn from your mistakes
   - Notice what you did well, and remember that you did your best

3. Someone close to you yells at you because you made a mistake. What would be helpful?
   - Notice the stress in your body and take a few deep breaths
   - Remember that everyone has difficult moments
   - Tell yourself that it's going to be okay
   - Shake off your stress
   - Remind yourself that you're still a good person

I think all of them could help me!

4. If your friend was feeling sad, what would be helpful?

- Notice how your friend is feeling and how you feel, too
- Remind them they're not alone
- Ask them if they'd like a hug, or let them know you care
- Ask them if they'd like to play a game or hang out
- Try to make them smile

5. You feel upset and your friend or parent asks you what's wrong. What would be helpful?

- Tell them how you are feeling
- Ask them if they've ever felt like this
- Ask them for a hug or some understanding
- Ask them to do something with you
- After sharing why you're upset, thank them for listening

6. A friend or sibling is better than you at something you have been trying hard to improve. What would be helpful?

- Notice how you feel
- Remind yourself that it takes time to grow skills
- Be an understanding friend to yourself
- Practice the skill you'd like to improve
- Tell yourself you are still doing great

Resilience Habit Animals

 = Buddy - I'm not alone / It's okay to feel this way

 = Spots - Noticing your five senses, feelings, or thoughts

= Sunny - Thinking of good things

 = Snuggles - Comforting or encouraging words or touch

 = Doodles - Actions that are kind to your body, mind or heart

For a more complete description of the resilience habits, you can look back at intro page XIII.

Count up the number of different animals that you chose.

You can add more resilience animal habits over time!

Activity 8.2 Resilience Presents

Buddy, Spots, Snuggles, and Doodles each have a box of resilience presents. Circle your favorite gifts from each resilience animal.

When you practice resilience habits, it's like you're giving Doodles a present!

Circle your favorite gifts from each resilience habit animal.

Remind yourself that…

- -Everyone struggles with something
- -You are not alone
- -Everyone makes mistakes and feels difficult feelings sometimes*
- -Everyone has strengths, including you!

The Buddy habit helps me the most. I remind myself that everyone makes mistakes.

- Notice and name your feelings
- 5 finger breathing (p.8)
- Notice sights, sounds, and other senses*
- Get curious about how your body feels*

"I like to use mindfulness (Spots) like noticing my senses or how I feel."
-Ambika, age 12

The Sunny habit helps me remember there are good things, too!
Sunny
- Cookie Breathing (p. 11)
- Notice and soak in good things
- Five finger gratitude (p. 8)
- Send kind wishes*
*These practices were taught in Volume 1.
- Treat yourself like a good friend*
- Give yourself kind words and comforting gestures
- Be an encouraging Inner Teammate
- Compassionate Friend Visualization (p. 25)
SUPER
Snuggles
"I like the Doodles habit of taking an action, like reading a book to calm myself down."
-Aarya, age 10
Doodles
- Stretch like an animal*
- Color or draw
- Move your body
- Take actions that are kind to your mind, body and heart
Shhhh... don't let Doodles know about the gifts yet.

Activity 8.3 Balloon Favorites

In the comic, James remembered different practices that had helped him in the past. You have learned so many ideas. Which ideas and practices have helped you? **You can pick your favorite idea from each animal or just decorate each balloon!**

Activity 8.4 A Card for Doodles

We've made it to our last activity! Let's get a little curious about our self-compassion journey. Are there some ways that you have grown and changed by doing the activities in this book?

You've learned so many practices and ideas! Doodles would love to hear about your adventures and your favorite resilience presents. You can look back at our adventures for ideas.

Tell Doodles about your favorite lands, and then draw a picture for your card.

Happy Birthday Doodles

Dear Doodles,

____

____

____

____

____

____

____

____

____

____

____

Love,

____

Your Signature Here

Adventure 8 Take-Aways

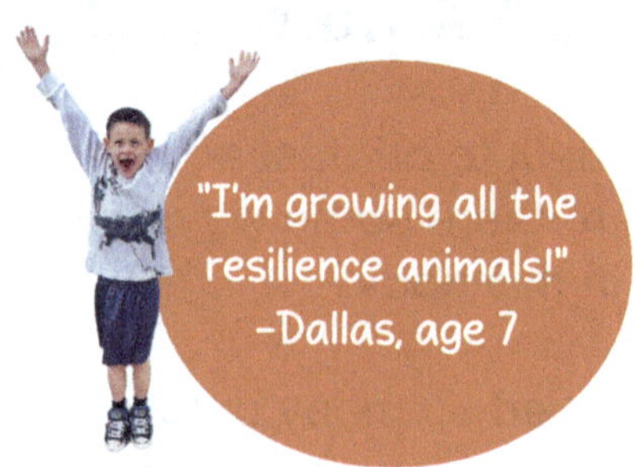

Resilience Habit Animals

 = Buddy - I'm not alone / It's okay to feel this way

 = Spots - Noticing your five senses, feelings, or thoughts

 = Sunny - Thinking of good things

 = Snuggles - Comforting or encouraging words or touch

 = Doodles - Actions that are kind to your body, mind or heart

Ideas and Practices:

 We need to practice self-compassion habits to grow resilience.

 Balance doing what is comfortable and trying new practices to help self-compassion feel less awkward.

Bonus Activity:

Habit Plan: It can be hard to remember to practice resilience habits, but there are a few things that can make remembering easier. It helps to plan a time and place to do your habits, and invite a grown-up to do it with you. You can use encouraging words to help each other grow new habits! You can do it!

Curiosity Question:

What resilience habit animal would you like to grow?

A Note for Grown-Ups:

What practices work best for you? Remember, growing your own self-compassion practice and modeling self-compassion for kids is one of the best ways to help kids grow self-compassion!

CELEBRATE
You made it! I am so proud of you!
Read the Scroll
Activity 8.1
Activity 8.2
Activity 8.3
Activity 8.4
Take-Aways
You are learning to practice resilience habits. HOORAY! Here are some sprinkles and a cupcake for our party.
GET READY TO PARTY!!

SURPRISE!!

Happy Birthday
to YOOOUU...
This is a dream
come true!

Certificate of Completion
Congratulations! The resilience animals are celebrating with you!
This certificate is presented to
For completing the
Quest for Self-Compassion

Acknowledgments:

I will forever be grateful to all of the children who helped me create this book!

I'm grateful to the kids in Milwaukee Public Schools who learned from this book in school–you inspire me to keep going. Thank you to the kids from the kids' team, especially Aarya for the many, many, MANY hours of helping me create and edit this book.

Special thanks to my daughters, Maya and Anjali, and my husband Patrick. Thank you for believing in me, listening to me talk endlessly about mindfulness and self-compassion, and supporting me when I worked many late nights to make this dream a reality.

Thank you to Kristin Neff and Christopher Germer, the creators of the Mindful Self-Compassion program, for inspiring me to teach self-compassion to children. And thank you to Karen Bluth for paving the way for bringing self-compassion to youth.

And thank you to each and every one of you. Your journey of self-compassion fills my heart with joy and gratitude. If your child enjoyed the adventures in this book, please give this book a review and share it with others. Our world truly needs this gift.

May our self-compassion practices continue to flourish and inspire others. We are in it together! ❤

Resources:

Free Companion Masterclass: how to help your child with perfectionism, inner criticism, and shame. https://jamielynntatera.com/workbook-for-kids-resources

Parent-Child Mindfulness and Self-Compassion Class: a playful course for kids ages 7–11 with a grown-up. https://jamielynntatera.com/parent-child-self-compassion-class/

Mindful Self-Compassion for Caregivers: grow your own resilience and self-compassion. https://jamielynntatera.com/classes-and-trainings/

More Resources: newsletter, videos, and articles with tips for helping your child. https://linktr.ee/jamielynntatera

Self-Compassion Resources from Kristin Neff, PhD: guided practices, meditations, and research. https://self-compassion.org/

Train to Teach Mindfulness and Self-Compassion to Kids: help more children learn self-compassion. https://jamielynntatera.com/train-to-teach/

References:

Germer, C., & Neff, K. (2018). *The Mindful Self-Compassion Workbook: A Proven Way to Accept Yourself, Build Inner Strength, and Thrive.* New York: Guilford Press.

Germer, C., & Neff, K. (2019). *Teaching the Mindful Self-Compassion Program: A Guide for Professionals.* New York: Harper Collins.

Tatera, J. 2020. Teacher Guide for the Mindfulness and Self-Compassion for Children and Caregivers Program (available for trained Mindfulness and Self-Compassion for Children and Caregivers teachers).

Tatera, J. (2020). *The Path to Resilience Photo Book*. Milwaukee, WI: Wholly Mindful, LLC.

About the Author:

Jamie Lynn Tatera is passionate about helping kids and grown-ups learn resilience and self-compassion skills. She is an elementary school educator, a certified Mindful Self-Compassion teacher, and the creator of the Mindfulness and Self-Compassion for Children and Caregivers (MSC-CC) program, which is a parent-child adaptation of the Mindful Self-Compassion course. She trains parents, educators and clinicians in her resiliency programs: https://jamielynntatera.com.

Jamie Lynn lives in Shorewood, Wisconsin, with her husband and two daughters, Maya and Anjali. When Jamie Lynn is not writing and teaching, she enjoys dancing, doing yoga, and spending time in nature.

About the Illustrators:

Alexis Warshall is a MIAD graduate who loves creating fun and whimsical art. She loves spending time outside with nature and her animals.

Alyssa Brown is an illustrator and storyteller from the Great Lakes Region. She loves telling stories and sharing them with others. When she isn't working on book layouts she is illustrating picture books. You can find her at https://www.alyssabrown.net

Thank you for helping me face my fears and grow my self-compassion!

Made in the USA
Coppell, TX
15 January 2026

69158189R00090